Fighting Transnational Bribery in Croatia

ASSESSMENT OF LEGAL AND POLICY FRAMEWORKS

OECD

BETTER POLICIES FOR BETTER LIVES

This work is published under the responsibility of the Secretary-General of the OECD. The opinions expressed and arguments employed herein do not necessarily reflect the official views of the Member countries of the OECD.

The project "Raising awareness and standards of fighting bribery in international business transactions" was co-funded by the European Union via the Structural Reform Support Programme (REFORM/IM2020/004). This publication was produced with the financial assistance of the European Union. The views expressed herein can in no way be taken to reflect the official opinion of the European Union.

This document, as well as any data and map included herein, are without prejudice to the status of or sovereignty over any territory, to the delimitation of international frontiers and boundaries and to the name of any territory, city or area.

The statistical data for Israel are supplied by and under the responsibility of the relevant Israeli authorities. The use of such data by the OECD is without prejudice to the status of the Golan Heights, East Jerusalem and Israeli settlements in the West Bank under the terms of international law.

Note by Turkey
The information in this document with reference to "Cyprus" relates to the southern part of the Island. There is no single authority representing both Turkish and Greek Cypriot people on the Island. Turkey recognises the Turkish Republic of Northern Cyprus (TRNC). Until a lasting and equitable solution is found within the context of the United Nations, Turkey shall preserve its position concerning the "Cyprus issue".

Note by all the European Union Member States of the OECD and the European Union
The Republic of Cyprus is recognised by all members of the United Nations with the exception of Turkey. The information in this document relates to the area under the effective control of the Government of the Republic of Cyprus.

Please cite this publication as:
OECD (2022), *Fighting Transnational Bribery in Croatia: Assessment of Legal and Policy Frameworks*, OECD Publishing, Paris, https://doi.org/10.1787/90d486ae-en.

ISBN 978-92-64-97052-6 (print)
ISBN 978-92-64-64193-8 (pdf)
ISBN 978-92-64-64342-0 (HTML)
ISBN 978-92-64-91389-9 (epub)

Foreword

In a globalised economy, efforts by countries to fight bribery in international business are ever more important to maintain a level playing field and ensure the integrity of international markets. This report assesses Croatia's legal and policy framework for fighting transnational bribery based on the criteria applied to countries seeking accession to the OECD Convention on Combating Bribery of Foreign Public Officials in International Business Transactions.

The report analyses Croatia's criminal legislation and the sanctions applicable to individuals and legal entities that commit bribery. It examines Croatia's track record in the investigation and prosecution of corruption offences and the overall enforcement framework. Rules on international co-operation (mutual legal assistance and extradition) as well as the non-tax deductibility of bribes are also examined. For each area of analysis, the report identifies areas for improvement and provides recommendations.

The report was prepared at the request of the Croatian authorities under a project supported financially by the European Commission Directorate General for Structural Reform Support (DG REFORM), and implemented with the active support of the Ministry of Justice and Public Administration of the Republic of Croatia.

Table of contents

FIGURES

Follow OECD Publications on:

http://twitter.com/OECD_Pubs

http://www.facebook.com/OECDPublications

http://www.linkedin.com/groups/OECD-Publications-4645871

http://www.youtube.com/oecdilibrary

http://www.oecd.org/oecddirect/

Abbreviations and acronyms

Art.	Article
CA	Criminal Act
CLL	Corporate Liability Law (Act on the Responsibility of Legal Persons for Criminal Offences)
CPA	Criminal Procedure Act
EU	European Union
EUR	Euro
HRK	Croatian kuna
MLA	Mutual legal assistance
MLACMA	Mutual Legal Assistance in Criminal Matters Act
OECD	Organisation for Economic Co-operation and Development
PNUSKOK	National Police Office for the Suppression of Corruption and Organised Crime
SME	Micro, small or medium-sized enterprise
SOE	State-owned or controlled enterprise
USKOK	Office for the Suppression of Corruption and Organised Crime

Executive summary

Croatia has expressed an interest in acceding to the OECD Anti-Bribery Convention and joining the international community's efforts to fight transnational bribery. This report, which was prepared at the request of the Croatian authorities, provides an assessment of Croatia's legal and policy framework for fighting transnational bribery in light of OECD standards, and identifies areas for improvement.

Key findings

Croatia's legislative and institutional framework for fighting transnational bribery meets many of the elements required by the OECD anti-bribery instruments. Legislation could be further improved to be fully aligned with these instruments. Croatian authorities also have a track record of domestic bribery enforcement, including in high-level corruption cases. However, enforcement against legal persons for bribery offences is lacking. Croatia has yet to investigate a transnational bribery case.

The review of Croatia's anti-bribery framework resulted in the following main findings:

- Croatian companies are active in countries with substantial levels of corruption, and are thus at risk of committing foreign bribery. However, Croatian stakeholders may not be completely aware of or agree with this foreign bribery risk profile for the country.

- Croatia's criminal legislation, which covers both domestic and foreign bribery, contains many of the essential features required by the OECD Anti-Bribery Convention. However, these provisions do not appear to cover certain elements of the foreign bribery offence as defined in the Convention, and could therefore be further expanded or clarified.

- Croatia provides for the liability of legal persons for foreign bribery and meets many of the standards demanded by the OECD Anti-Bribery Convention. However, some of the criteria for triggering entities' liability appear too narrow and could be expanded.

- Croatia provides a range of sanctions against natural and legal persons for foreign bribery, including imprisonment (for natural persons), fines, confiscation and debarment. To further improve this regime, Croatia could consider increasing the maximum fines available against natural and legal persons for foreign bribery, and ensuring that the sanctions imposed in practice are effective, proportionate and dissuasive.

- Croatia has a track record of enforcing domestic bribery offences against natural persons, including in high-level corruption cases. There is no such similar enforcement for foreign bribery, however. Also absent is enforcement against legal persons for foreign and domestic bribery. Croatia could therefore enhance enforcement of domestic and foreign bribery against natural and legal persons where appropriate.

- Despite the existence of formal guarantees of judicial and prosecutorial independence, EU data show that the level of perceived judicial independence among companies and the general public is low. Croatian stakeholders in the judiciary and law enforcement are more positive about judicial independence, however. The EU data also show considerable delay in criminal proceedings. Some Croatian stakeholders suggest that this fuels a public perception that enforcement is selective and favours low-level corruption. Croatia could therefore consider taking steps to reduce delay in criminal proceedings in corruption cases.

- Croatia has treaty relations in extradition and MLA with many foreign countries. In the absence of an applicable treaty, these are available on the basis of reciprocity. The report identifies a few areas in which Croatia could further improve its international co-operation system.

- Croatia prohibits the tax deduction of bribes through a range of provisions in the tax legislation. To strengthen its framework, Croatia could consider enacting an explicit, legally binding provision on the non-deductibility of bribes.

1 Recommendations for fighting transnational bribery in Croatia

This chapter summarises the recommendations covered in the report for fighting transnational bribery in Croatia.

In light of this report's analysis, Croatia is recommended to take the following steps to strengthen its legal and enforcement framework for fighting foreign bribery:

1. With respect to the <u>foreign bribery offence</u>, Croatia could:

    i. Take steps to ensure that the offence's intent requirement is sufficiently broad to cover typical foreign bribery transactions, in particular bribery committed through intermediaries.

    ii. Expand the definition of a foreign public official, including to persons who hold legislative office in or who exercise a public function for a foreign country; employees of foreign state-owned or controlled enterprises; and officials of all public international organisations, including those in which Croatia is not a member.

    iii. Ensure that the definition of a foreign public official is autonomous and does not require proof of foreign law.

    iv. Clarify that the definition of a foreign country includes "all levels and subdivisions of government, from national to local", as well as any organised foreign area or entity, such as an autonomous territory or a separate customs territory.

2. With respect to the <u>liability of legal persons</u> for foreign bribery, Croatia could take steps to ensure that liability can result from all acts of foreign bribery, and not only those that result in an "illegal property gain" to the legal person.

3. Regarding <u>sanctions</u> for foreign bribery, Croatia could:

    i. Increase the maximum fines available against natural and legal persons for foreign bribery.

    ii. Take steps to ensure that the sanctions imposed against natural and legal persons in practice are effective, proportionate and dissuasive.

    iii. Maintain detailed statistics on the sanctions, including on the amount of fines, as well as on confiscation and debarment that have been imposed in domestic and foreign bribery cases.

4. With respect to foreign bribery <u>enforcement</u>, Croatia could:

    i. Enhance enforcement of the domestic and foreign bribery offences against natural and legal persons whenever appropriate.

    ii. Take steps to reduce delay in criminal proceedings in corruption cases.

5. Regarding <u>international co-operation in foreign bribery cases</u>, Croatia could:

    i. Provide a broad range of MLA, including coercive measures, in foreign bribery-related civil or administrative proceedings against a legal person to a foreign state whose legal system does not allow criminal liability of legal persons.

    ii. Ensure that MLA is not refused because of *ne bis in idem* in cases in which criminal proceedings in Croatia have been discontinued on grounds other than the merits.

    iii. Ensure that cases that are declined for extradition solely on grounds of nationality are submitted to prosecution.

6. Regarding the <u>non-tax deductibility of bribes</u>, Croatia could enact an explicit, legally binding provision prohibiting such deductions.

2 Introduction

This chapter introduces the project under which the report was prepared, as well as the report methodology. It then illustrates the main OECD anti-bribery instruments and the criteria for countries' accession to the OECD Anti-Bribery Convention.

2.1. Raising awareness and standards of fighting bribery in international business transactions

In the age of a globalised economy, fighting bribery in international business is ever more important to maintain a level playing field and ensure the integrity of international markets. This is especially pertinent to countries in the European single market like Croatia. Foreign bribery raises serious moral and political concerns, undermines good governance and economic development, and distorts international competitive conditions. All countries share a responsibility to combat this crime. The OECD Convention on Combating Bribery of Foreign Public Officials in International Business Transactions (OECD, 1997[1]) (Anti-Bribery Convention) is the only international treaty dedicated to fighting transnational bribery in business.

Croatia has expressed an interest in acceding to the Anti-Bribery Convention and joining the international community's efforts to fight transnational bribery. In this context, the project "Raising Awareness and Standards of Fighting Bribery in International Business Transactions" was jointly conducted by Croatia's Ministry of Justice and Public Administration, the European Commission, and the Organisation for Economic Co-operation and Development (OECD). The project was financed by the European Union Structural Reform Support Programme.

The purpose of the project is to strengthen Croatia's anti-corruption framework towards the standards set out in the OECD Anti-Bribery Convention. The project also supports Croatia's initiatives to develop adequate systemic anti-corruption interventions related to the private sector and combating bribery in international business, making these efforts one of the priority areas in its national anti-corruption strategy. Indeed, Croatia's Anti-Corruption Strategy for 2021-2030 mentions this project as part of the policy priority of "Strengthening the institutional and normative framework for the fight against corruption".[1] "Improving anti-bribery frameworks in international business transactions" is one of the measures for implementing the strategy.

To accomplish these goals, the project comprises three components. First, Croatia's legal and policy framework for fighting the bribery of foreign public officials is assessed against OECD standards and areas for improvement are identified. This report is the output of this project component. Second, a one-day event is held to raise awareness of the importance of fighting bribery in international business transactions. The goal is to secure the commitment of key stakeholders in Croatia in this important endeavour. Finally, workshops are held to present the assessment of Croatia's legal and policy framework, and to mobilise support for implementing the OECD's recommendations.

2.2. Methodology

The present report assesses Croatia's legal and policy framework for fighting transnational bribery based on the criteria applied to countries seeking accession to the Anti-Bribery Convention. These criteria have been defined by the OECD Working Group on Bribery in International Business Transactions, which is the Convention's Conference of Parties.[2] The criteria focus on a subset of key requirements of the Anti-Bribery Convention. An assessment based on these criteria is thus more limited than the regular country evaluations conducted by the Working Group, which monitor the implementation of the entire Convention. The present report is prepared by the OECD Secretariat and published under the authority of the OECD Secretary-General. The assessment contained therein reflects the views of the OECD Secretariat and not necessarily the OECD Working Group on Bribery or its member countries. The assessment is without prejudice to any subsequent evaluation of Croatia that may be conducted by the Working Group.

The assessment in the present report relies on multiple sources of information. At the outset, Croatian authorities responded to a questionnaire prepared by the OECD Secretariat. The OECD then conducted a fact-finding mission to gather additional information. The mission comprised panels with relevant

Croatian stakeholders including government officials, prosecutors, judges, parliamentarians, private-sector lawyers and academics, private sector and civil society (see Annex A for a list of participants). The mission was conducted virtually via teleconference because of travel restrictions necessitated by the COVID-19 pandemic. After the mission, Croatian authorities provided additional information and commented on a draft of this report. The OECD Secretariat also conducted independent research. The OECD is grateful to Croatian authorities and all participants of the fact-finding mission for their openness and generosity with their time.

2.3. OECD Anti-Bribery Convention

The OECD's main anti-bribery instruments are the Anti-Bribery Convention and the 2021 Anti-Bribery Recommendation. In 2013, the OECD Working Group on Bribery set out the criteria for countries to accede and adhere to these instruments.

The OECD's flagship anti-bribery instrument is the Anti-Bribery Convention (OECD, 1997[1]). The Convention was adopted in 1997 and entered into force in 1999. At the time of this report, there are 44 Parties to the Convention, i.e. 38 OECD members and 6 non-members.[3] The Convention (Art. 1) requires Parties to criminalise the bribery of foreign public officials (foreign bribery) committed by natural persons. Legal persons must also be made liable for this crime (Art. 2). Natural and legal persons that are culpable must be subject to effective, proportionate and dissuasive sanctions (Art. 3). Parties must seriously investigate foreign bribery allegations implicating their nationals and companies. These enforcement actions must also be independent of executive influence, as well as considerations of national economic interest, the potential effect upon relations with another state or the identity of the natural or legal persons involved (Art. 5). Parties must also provide mutual legal assistance and extradition in foreign bribery cases (Arts. 9 and 10).

2.4. 2021 and 2009 Anti-Bribery Recommendations

The Anti-Bribery Convention is complemented by the 2021 Recommendation of the Council for Further Combating Bribery of Foreign Public Officials in International Business Transactions (OECD, 2021[2]). The Recommendation is an update of an earlier version adopted in 2009 (OECD, 2009[3]). Countries that accede to the Anti-Bribery Convention are also required to adhere to the Anti-Bribery Recommendation. The 2021 Recommendation provides additional guidance on implementing the foreign bribery offence and corporate liability for this crime (Annex I). It sets out measures for preventing, detecting and reporting foreign bribery. It also urges countries to fully and promptly implement the 2009 Council Recommendation on Tax Measures for Further Combating Bribery of Foreign Public Officials in International Business Transactions (OECD, 2009[4]). In particular, countries are recommended to "explicitly disallow the tax deductibility of bribes to foreign public officials, for all tax purposes in an effective manner".

2.5. Criteria for acceding to the Anti-Bribery Convention

In 2013, the OECD Working Group on Bribery adopted the current criteria and procedure for a country to accede to the Anti-Bribery Convention and to become a Working Group Member.[4] The criteria fall into three categories: (1) economic factors relevant for assessing "mutual interest"; (2) factors relating to the legal and enforcement framework to fight foreign bribery; and (3) factors relating to the willingness and ability to participate in the Working Group's work programme.

2.5.1. Criteria relating to economic factors for assessing "mutual interest"

Accession is of "mutual interest" if it assists the OECD Working Group on Bribery in fulfilling its mandate of combating foreign bribery. This mandate includes an objective to "engage with non-Member countries that are major exporters and foreign investors, with a view to their adherence and implementation of [the OECD anti-bribery] instruments". In assessing "mutual interest", the Working Group considers the following economic indicators:[5]

  a   The size of the accession candidate's economy as measured by its gross domestic product (GDP);

  b   The volume of the accession candidate's trade, including imports and exports, and in goods and services, subject to the availability of data;

  c   The accession candidate's stock of outward foreign direct investment (FDI);

  d   The accession candidate's level of trade with and FDI stocks in countries with perceived high levels of corruption; and

  e   The proportion of companies in the accession candidate that operate in sectors shown to be a serious foreign bribery risk, e.g. extractive industries, defence, and infrastructure.

The Working Group applies these economic criteria flexibly. Accordingly, the economic indicators of an accession candidate would not be required to meet particular thresholds, nor would any one or more factors be determinative. Instead, the Working Group considers all relevant factors as a whole to determine whether a country's accession would be of mutual interest to the candidate and the Working Group.

2.5.2. Criteria relating to the legal and enforcement framework to fight foreign bribery

An adequate legal and enforcement framework is essential for combating foreign bribery effectively. The OECD Working Group on Bribery's criteria for accession to the Convention thus focus on the following six factors relating to a country's legal and enforcement framework:[6]

  a   Foreign bribery offence: The Working Group considers whether an accession candidate has a criminal offence that specifically and expressly criminalises foreign bribery. The Working Group further assesses an accession candidate's foreign bribery offence against Art. 1 of the Convention and Annex I of the 2009 Recommendation.[7]

  b   Liability of legal persons for foreign bribery: The Working Group considers whether an accession candidate has the ability to impose criminal, civil, and/or administrative liability against legal persons for foreign bribery. A general scheme that allows liability to be imposed for intentional criminal offences would suffice, i.e. the scheme does not have to be specific to foreign bribery. The Working Group further assesses an accession candidate's scheme for imposing liability against legal persons for foreign bribery against Art. 2 of the Convention and Annex I of the 2009 Recommendation.

  c   Sanctions for foreign bribery: The Working Group assesses the sanctions available for foreign bribery against Art. 3 of the Convention, and the sanctions imposed in practice for foreign and domestic bribery.

  d   Enforcement capacity: The capacity to enforce foreign bribery laws is a key indicator of the importance given to tackling foreign bribery. The Working Group therefore considers the following two criteria:

   i.   Whether an accession candidate has a track record of investigating and prosecuting (domestic and foreign) corruption cases. This could be measured by considering investigations and prosecutions over a previous five-year period. Particular emphasis would be given to foreign bribery cases; politically sensitive cases; cases impacting national economic interests; enforcement actions for active (as opposed to passive) corruption; and enforcement actions against legal persons; and

ii. Any other matter relevant to the candidate's capacity to enforce its foreign bribery laws that comes to the Working Group's attention and which raises significant concerns, *e.g.* well-publicised interference by the executive government in an investigation, or the abolition of an anti-corruption agency.

e International co-operation: The Working Group assesses an accession candidate's legal and legislative framework for seeking and providing mutual legal assistance (MLA) and extradition against Arts. 9 and 10 of the Convention. The Working Group also considers any other information that comes to its attention and which is relevant to the candidate's capacity to seek and provide MLA and extradition.

f Explicit non-tax deductibility of bribes: The Working Group considers whether an accession candidate explicitly disallows the tax deductibility of bribes to foreign public officials for all tax purposes.

2.5.3. Criteria relating to the willingness and ability to participate in the Working Group on Bribery's work programme

The last category of criteria for acceding to the Anti-Bribery Convention concerns a country's willingness and ability to participate in the work programme of the OECD Working Group on Bribery, and to fulfil Convention obligations that go beyond legal and enforcement issues. These criteria include an assessment of a candidate country's ability to co-operate in the Working Group's accession review process and other review mechanisms; participation in the Working Group as a non-member, and the procedure and time (including possible limits) for accession.[8] Since these criteria do not relate to a country's legal and policy framework, they are beyond the scope of this report.

References

OECD (2021), *2021 Recommendation of the Council for Further Combating Bribery of Foreign Public Officials in International Business Transactions*, https://www.oecd.org/daf/anti-bribery/2021-oecd-anti-bribery-recommendation.htm. [2]

OECD (2009), *2009 Recommendation of the Council for Further Combating Bribery of Foreign Public Officials in International Business Transactions*, https://www.oecd.org/daf/anti-bribery/ConvCombatBribery_ENG.pdf. [3]

OECD (2009), *Recommendation of the Council on Tax Measures for Further Combating Bribery of Foreign Public Officials in International Business Transactions*, https://legalinstruments.oecd.org/en/instruments/OECD-LEGAL-0286#dates. [4]

OECD (1997), *OECD Convention on Combating Bribery of Foreign Public Officials in International Business Transactions*, https://www.oecd.org/corruption/oecdantibriberyconvention.htm. [1]

Notes

[1] Anti-Corruption Strategy for 2021-2030 (*Strategija sprječavanja korupcije za razdoblje od 2021. do 2030. godine*), Official Gazette No. 120/21, Section 4.1 and Annex 1, Measure 4.1.12.

[2] OECD Working Group on Bribery in International Business Transactions (2014), "Criteria and Procedure for Acceding to the Anti-Bribery Convention and Non-Member Participation in the Working Group on Bribery" (Accession Criteria), DAF/WGB(2014)2/FINAL.

[3] The 38 OECD members are Austria, Australia, Belgium, Canada, Chile, Colombia, Costa Rica, Czech Republic, Denmark, Estonia, Finland, France, Germany, Greece, Hungary, Iceland, Ireland, Israel, Italy, Japan, Korea, Latvia, Lithuania, Luxembourg, Mexico, the Netherlands, New Zealand, Norway, Poland, Portugal, Slovak Republic, Slovenia, Spain, Sweden, Switzerland, Turkey, the United Kingdom and the United States. The 6 non-OECD countries that are Parties to the Convention are Argentina, Brazil, Bulgaria, Peru, Russian Federation and South Africa.

[4] Accession Criteria, DAF/WGB(2014)2/FINAL.

[5] Accession Criteria, para. 9.

[6] Accession Criteria, para. 11.

[7] The Working Group adopted its Accession Criteria in 2013, before the 2009 Anti-Bribery Recommendation was updated in 2021. At the time of this report, the Working Group has not yet discussed a revision to the Accession Criteria to account for the updated 2021 Anti-Bribery Recommendation.

[8] Accession Criteria, para. 12.

3 Croatia's economic profile and risk of foreign bribery

This chapter provides a brief introduction of Croatia's economic profile, with a particular focus on the indicators that can offer information on Croatian companies' exposure to risks of foreign bribery, such as exports and foreign direct investments.

As mentioned in Section 2.5.1, the first category of criteria for accession to the OECD Anti-Bribery Convention considers a range of economic indicators in a country. The OECD Working Group on Bribery examines these indicators to determine whether accession to the Anti-Bribery Convention is of "mutual interest" to the Working Group and the country seeking accession.

Croatia has a population of approximately 4.3 million. It joined the European Union in 2013 but is not in the euro zone or the Schengen area. If it were a member of the OECD Working Group on Bribery, then it would have the 40th largest economy out of 45 member countries. In terms of GDP per capita, it would rank 35th.[1]

In terms of trade, Croatia would rank 40th out of 45 Working Group members in both exports and imports of merchandise. The main exports are machinery and transport equipment, accounting for almost one quarter of the total (23.9%), followed by manufactured goods classified chiefly by material (17.1%) and miscellaneous manufactured articles (13.8%). The top five export destinations are Germany (13.1%), Italy (12.6%), Slovenia (10.4%), Bosnia and Herzegovina (8.6%), and Hungary (6.8%). Germany is also the biggest import source (15.4%), followed by Italy (12.5%), Slovenia (11.4%), Hungary (7.8%) and Austria (6.7%). The main imports are machinery and transport equipment (26.0%), manufactured goods classified by material (18.2%), and chemical products (16.9%).[2]

As for foreign direct investment (FDI), Croatia would rank last out of 45 Working Group countries in terms of outward FDI stocks, and 40th for inward FDI stocks. The largest destination countries are Bosnia and Herzegovina (27.8%), Slovenia (22.5%), Serbia (19.1%), Montenegro (6.1%), and Poland (4.2%). The main sources of inward FDI are Austria (13.9%), Netherlands (13.2%), Luxembourg (11.3%), Germany (10.8%) and Italy (10.4%).[3]

State-owned enterprises (SOEs) play a significant role in Croatia's economy. The country has one of the highest number of SOEs per capita in the EU, including in central and south-Eastern Europe. The central government holds full or majority ownership in 59 SOEs (including 6 listed companies) and minority stakes in 10 listed companies. The SOE sector (including at the sub-national level) is valued at 47.2% of GDP and accounts for 6.5% of total employment. The sectors with the most SOEs include transportation and storage; finance; manufacturing; construction; telecommunication; electricity and gas; agriculture, forestry and fishing; and real estate.[4]

Micro-, small- and medium-sized enterprises (SMEs) represent a substantial part of the economy and are active internationally. In 2019, SMEs accounted for 59.4% of value added and 68.9% of employment in Croatia's "non-financial business economy", both above EU averages.[5] The Croatian government has made a concerted effort to seek overseas markets for SMEs, ranking 3rd of 28 EU countries in 2018 in the internationalisation of SMEs.[6] That same year, Croatian SMEs accounted for 53.0% of the country's exports.[7]

Croatian companies, including SOEs, are active in countries with substantial levels of corruption and are thus exposed to risks of foreign bribery. One-sixth of Croatia's exports are to members of the Central European Free Trade Agreement, which consist of mostly of countries in South Eastern Europe (World Trade Organisation, n.d.[1]). Among Croatia's major trade and investment destinations, several rank poorly on Transparency International Corruption Perception Index 2020 (Transparency International, 2020[2]), including Bosnia and Herzegovina (111th out of 180 countries), North Macedonia (tied for 111th), Serbia (94th) and Montenegro (67th). These four countries alone account for 55.3% of Croatia's outward FDI stock and 15.4% of exports in merchandise. Some Croatian SOEs operating in these countries are active in risk sectors such as energy and extractive industries.[8]

However, Croatian stakeholders may not be completely aware of or agree with this foreign bribery risk profile for the country. Private sector representatives at the fact-finding mission state that they are unaware of any instances of foreign bribery involving Croatian companies. Parliamentarians state that foreign bribery is "generally not a problem" and that Croatian companies are not sufficiently large and hence cannot afford to bribe foreign officials. Only civil society representatives acknowledge a risk of Croatian companies bribing abroad.

References

CEPOR (2019), *Small and Medium Enterprises Report: Croatia 2019*, http://www.cepor.hr/wp-content/uploads/2015/03/SME-REPORT-2019-EN-WEB.pdf. [4]

OECD (2021), *OECD Review of the Corporate Governance of State-Owned Enterprises in Croatia*, https://www.oecd.org/corporate/soe-review-croatia.htm. [3]

Transparency International (2020), *Corruption Perceptions Index*, https://www.transparency.org/en/cpi/2020/. [2]

World Trade Organisation (n.d.), *WTO Data - Information on trade and trade policy measures*, https://data.wto.org/en. [1]

Notes

[1] Croatia.eu; International Monetary Fund, 2020 GDP in constant prices and GDP per capita at purchasing power parity.

[2] Information provided by Croatian authorities. Additional information obtained from the World Trade Organisation database and Trade Profile 2020.

[3] Croatian National Bank and UNCTADStat.

[4] (OECD, 2021[3]), Part I, Sections 2.1-2.2.

[5] European Commission (2019), SBA Fact Sheet: Croatia.

[6] European Commission (2019), SBA Fact Sheet & Scoreboard.

[7] (CEPOR, 2019[4]), p. 14.

[8] (OECD, 2021[3]), Part I, Section 4.2.

4 Foreign bribery offence

This chapter analyses the provisions of Croatia's Criminal Act to determine whether all the elements of the offence of bribery of foreign public officials as defined in the OECD Anti-Bribery Convention are adequately covered in Croatia's legislation.

The offence of foreign bribery is the first Convention accession criterion on the legal and enforcement framework to fight foreign bribery. Under the accession methodology, the OECD Working Group on Bribery assesses an accession candidate's foreign bribery offence against Convention Art. 1 and the 2009 Recommendation Annex I.

4.1. OECD standards on the foreign bribery offence

Art. 1(1) of the Convention sets out the requirements of a foreign bribery offence:

> *Article 1:*
>
> *The Offence of Bribery of Foreign Public Officials:*
>
> *Each Party shall take such measures as may be necessary to establish that it is a criminal offence under its law for any person intentionally to offer, promise or give any undue pecuniary or other advantage, whether directly or through intermediaries, to a foreign public official, for that official or for a third party, in order that the official act or refrain from acting in relation to the performance of official duties, in order to obtain or retain business or other improper advantage in the conduct of international business.*

Additional guidance on the foreign bribery offence is found in Commentaries 3-19 of the Convention, and Annex I.A of the 2009 Anti-Bribery Recommendation.

4.2. Croatia's foreign bribery offence

Croatia's foreign bribery offence is in Art. 294 of the Criminal Act (CA).[1] Art. 294(1) deals with bribery in order that an official do or omit to do something that he/she should not. This is known as bribery *in breach of* one's duties in some countries. Art. 294(2) covers bribery *to perform* one's duties, i.e. to induce an official to do or omit to do something that he/she should. Art. 294(3) releases the briber from punishment under certain circumstances:

> *Article 294*
>
> *Giving bribes*
>
> *(1) Whoever offers, gives or promises a bribe intended to that or another person to an official or responsible person to perform within or outside the limits of his authority an official or other action which he should not perform or not to perform an official or other action which he should perform, or whoever mediates in such bribery of an official or responsible person shall be punished by imprisonment for a term between one and eight years.*
>
> *(2) Whoever offers, gives or promises a bribe intended to that or another person to an official or responsible person to perform an official or other action that he should perform, or not to perform an official or other action that he should not perform, within or outside the limits of his authority, or whoever mediates in such bribery of an official or responsible person shall be punished by imprisonment for a term between six months and five years.*
>
> *(3) The perpetrator of the criminal offence referred to in paragraphs 1 and 2 of this Article who gave a bribe at the request of an official or responsible person and reported the offence before its discovery or before learning that the offence was discovered, may be released from punishment.*

4.3. Elements of the foreign bribery offence

Under the accession methodology, the assessment of an accession candidate's foreign bribery offence is comparable to a Working Group Phase 1 evaluation of Parties to the Convention (OECD, n.d.[1]). Each discrete element of the candidate's foreign bribery offence is measured against the Convention and 2009 Recommendation. These elements are analysed below.

4.3.1. Any person

Convention Art. 1(1) requires a foreign bribery offence to apply to "any person". The offence in CA Art. 294 applies to "whoever" commits bribery. Croatian authorities state that the offence applies to "anyone" (*delicta communia*).

4.3.2. Intentionally

Convention Art. 1(1) covers foreign bribery committed "intentionally".

CA Art. 28 provides that crimes, including the foreign bribery offence in CA Art. 294, may be committed with direct or indirect intent. An individual has direct intent when he/she is aware of the material elements of the criminal offence, and wants or is sure of the elements' realisation. Indirect intent exists when an individual is aware that he/she is capable of realising the material elements of the offence, and accedes to their realisation.

A common issue is whether the intent requirement of a foreign bribery offence is sufficiently broad to cover a typical foreign bribery transaction. Such a transaction could involve an entrepreneur who pays a consultant a large sum of money. The consultant is asked to "do whatever it takes" to win a public procurement contract for the individual in a foreign country with widespread corruption. The consultant does not provide any other tangible work product or services in return. The entrepreneur also does not question how the consultant would spend the large sum of money that he/she receives. The entrepreneur is therefore wilfully blind to whether the consultant would use the money to bribe an official in the foreign country in order to win the contract.

Croatian prosecutors at the fact-finding mission do not believe that the foreign bribery offence would readily cover this typical foreign bribery transaction. They state that bribery is usually committed with direct intent and rarely with indirect intent. In the hypothetical situation above, there must be evidence that the entrepreneur is aware that the consultant would unlawfully influence foreign public officials. One prosecutor states that the entrepreneur must know what happens to the money. Another prosecutor explains that a conviction would require the consultant to explain to the entrepreneur that there is a "high likelihood" that the consultant has to bribe an official. The entrepreneur must then agree to this course of action. This conversation must also be proven through direct evidence, for example via a wiretap or video recording.

Fact-finding mission participants from the judiciary, legal profession and academia express similar views. A judge considers that there must be direct proof of an agreement to bribe between the entrepreneur and the consultant. It is difficult to convict an individual who "does not want to speak about the bribe". A professor states that the entrepreneur in the hypothetical above must know or accept that a bribe would be given. A defence lawyer adds that asking the consultant to "do whatever it takes" is ambiguous and not sufficient to establish indirect intent. A conversation – captured on wiretap – in which the entrepreneur and consultant state "we are ready to pay the bribe" would be necessary for a conviction.

Given these views, the intent requirement of Croatia's foreign bribery offence is likely too narrow. An entrepreneur must have a substantial level of knowledge of the bribery act before indirect intent is established. Moreover, direct rather than circumstantial evidence of knowledge is generally necessary to prove indirect and even direct intent. It would not be difficult for an individual to structure a foreign bribery transaction to circumvent these requirements for intent. The OECD Working Group on Bribery has therefore made recommendations to countries where the intent requirement or evidentiary threshold of foreign bribery offences is too onerous.[2]

The Croatian Ministry of Justice and Public Administration disagrees with these views. It states that, in the hypothetical situation above, a response to the entrepreneur's request to "do whatever it takes" depends on the wider context. Nevertheless, if the entrepreneur "is aware of the *possibility* that the consultant would use given money to commit a criminal offence of foreign bribery and agrees with that possibility", then the entrepreneur acts with the indirect intent and would be liable. Furthermore, wiretap evidence of the bribery agreement is "ideal" – i.e. not strictly necessary – for a conviction. However, these positions of the Ministry contradict those expressed by the fact-finding mission participants.

4.3.3. Offer, promise or give

CA Art. 294 mirrors Convention Art. 1(1) by covering someone who "offers, promises or gives" a bribe. Croatian authorities state that an offer occurs when an individual indicates a readiness to provide a bribe. A promise results when an individual agrees with an official to provide a bribe. Giving is the transfer of a bribe. Croatian authorities add that the offence is complete when the perpetrator undertakes one of these actions. Proof that the foreign public official received the bribe or acted as a result of the bribe is not required. Supporting case law or jurisprudence is not provided, however.

4.3.4. Any undue pecuniary or other advantage

Convention Art. 1(1) requires a foreign bribery offence to cover the giving, offer or promise of "any undue pecuniary or other advantage" to a foreign public official.

CA Art. 87(24) defines a bribe as "any undue reward, gift or other property or non-property benefit, regardless of value". Both pecuniary and non-pecuniary bribes are therefore covered. Croatian authorities add that the term "undue" refers to "an official who receives something that he/she should not", or a thing that "does not belong to the official".

4.3.5. Whether directly or through intermediaries

Convention Art. 1(1) requires a foreign bribery offence to cover the giving, offer or promise of a bribe to a foreign public official, "whether directly or through intermediaries". The OECD has noted that using intermediaries is one of the most common *modus operandi* of the crime of foreign bribery (OECD, 2020[2]; 2009[3]).

CA Art. 294 does not explicitly cover bribery through an intermediary. However, CA Art. 36 provides that a person who commits an offence "through another person" shall be liable as a principal. Furthermore, liability as co-perpetrators arises if several persons commit an offence based on a joint decision, and each participates or significantly contributes to the commission of the offence. The offence in CA Art. 294 also expressly provides for liability of the intermediary. Case law or jurisprudence on bribery through intermediaries is not provided, however. As discussed in Section 4.3.2, the intent requirement of Croatia's foreign bribery offence may limit the liability of bribery through intermediaries.

4.3.6. A foreign public official

Definitions in the Anti-Bribery Convention and Croatian law

Art. 1(4)(a) of the Convention defines a "foreign public official":

Article 1(4) For the purpose of this Convention:

(a) "foreign public official" means any person holding a legislative, administrative or judicial office of a foreign country, whether appointed or elected; any person exercising a public function for a foreign country, including for a public agency or public enterprise; and any official or agent of a public international organisation.

Croatia's CA Art. 294 prohibits the bribery of an "official", a term that is defined in CA Art. 87(3). In sum, the provision defines an "official" to include certain Croatian officials. It then extends this definition to persons who perform the same functions in foreign states, international organisations etc.:

Article 87(3) An official is a state official or civil servant, an official or clerk in a unit of local and regional self-government, a holder of judicial office, a lay judge, a member of the State Judicial Council or the State Attorney's Council, an arbitrator, a notary public and a professional worker performing tasks of social work, education and training activities. An official is also a person who in the European Union, a foreign state, an international organisation of which the Republic of Croatia is a member, an international court or arbitration tribunal whose jurisdiction the Republic of Croatia accepts, performs duties entrusted to persons referred to in the previous sentence.

CA Art. 294 also prohibits the bribery of a "responsible person", which is defined in CA Art. 87(6). Of note, this latter provision does not explicitly extend the definition of a "responsible person" to individuals with equivalent functions in a foreign state or international organisation:

Article 87(6) A responsible person is a natural person who manages the affairs of a legal person or is explicitly or actually entrusted with the performance of activities in the field of activity of a legal person or state bodies or bodies of a local and regional self-government unit.

Croatia's Ministry of Justice and Public Administration contends that a "responsible person" can be a foreign public official but this is unlikely. It states that a "responsible person" can be a *Croatian citizen or resident* by reason of CA Art. 14(1), which provides for jurisdiction over Croatian nationals for extraterritorial crimes. However, a Croatian national or resident is unlikely to be the foreign public official receiving a bribe in a foreign bribery case. Croatia also states that a "responsible person" can be a foreign citizen if a crime is committed on Croatian territory due to CA Art. 10. This is doubtful, since the provision deals with territorial jurisdiction of the Criminal Act and not the substantive definition of a "responsible person". But even if Croatia's position is correct, the provision would not apply to the vast majority of foreign bribery cases since the crime is often committed outside the briber's country.

Types of foreign public officials covered

Overall, there is some question over whether Croatia's definition fully covers all persons holding an administrative office of a foreign country. The definition of an "official" in CA Art. 87(3) explicitly covers "a holder of judicial office" and "a lay judge" in a foreign state. But there is no mention of holders of "administrative office". Such persons *in Croatia* may be covered as "responsible persons" under CA Art. 87(6). But as mentioned above, it is debatable whether "responsible persons" include officials of *foreign countries*.

The term "official" in Art. 87(3) also does not appear to cover holders of "legislative office", whether in Croatia, another country or an international organisation. Bribery of legislators is addressed in a separate offence in CA Art. 339. But this offence applies only to members of the Croatian Parliament, European Parliament, and councillors in the representative bodies of (Croatian) local and regional governments. Legislators in foreign countries and other international organisations are not included. However, Croatian authorities say that the definition of "official" in Art. 87(3) should be interpreted in light of the Act on Obligations and Rights of State Officials.[3] Under Art. 1 of the Act, "Officials within the meaning of the Act are [...] Members of the Croatian Parliament". This interpretation is debatable, as it would mean that two different offences (CA Arts. 294 and 339) with different ranges of possible penalties apply to the bribery of a Croatian Parliamentarian. Croatian authorities explain that this is because the offence in CA Art. 339

"covers actions which cannot be subsumed under [Arts. 293-294] due to the fact that voting of a representative cannot be understood as an official act. In this manner the Croatian legislator has fulfilled the aforesaid legal gap." But this implies that the "legal gap" remains for foreign legislative officials, since CA Art 339 does not apply to non-Croatian officials.

Similar questions arise about the coverage of "any person exercising a public function for a foreign country". Convention Commentary 12 explains that a "'public function' includes any activity in the public interest, delegated by a foreign country, such as the performance of a task delegated by it in connection with public procurement." One purpose of this provision is therefore to cover states that contract out certain public functions to private sector providers. However, the definition of an "official" in CA Art. 87(3) does not cover public functions generically. Instead, it describes specific types of functions or professions. The definition of a "responsible person" in CA Art. 87(6) is broader. The concept encompasses persons "entrusted with the performance of activities in the field of activity of a legal person or state bodies or bodies of a local and regional self-government unit". But as mentioned above, it is not clear that the provision applies to individuals in foreign states.

Employees of foreign state-owned or state-controlled enterprises

Convention Art. 1(4)(a) states that a "foreign public official" should include "any person exercising a public function for a foreign country, including for a public agency or public enterprise". A "public enterprise" is essentially a foreign state-owned or controlled enterprise (SOE), according to Commentary 14:

> Commentary 14. A "public enterprise" is any enterprise, regardless of its legal form, over which a government, or governments, may, directly or indirectly, exercise a dominant influence. This is deemed to be the case, inter alia, when the government or governments hold the majority of the enterprise's subscribed capital, control the majority of votes attaching to shares issued by the enterprise or can appoint a majority of the members of the enterprise's administrative or managerial body or supervisory board.

Commentary 15 adds that an SOE in a privileged market position is deemed to be performing a public function:

> Commentary 15. An official of a public enterprise shall be deemed to perform a public function unless the enterprise operates on a normal commercial basis in the relevant market, i.e., on a basis which is substantially equivalent to that of a private enterprise, without preferential subsidies or other privileges.

Examples of such enterprises may therefore include a majority state-owned aircraft manufacturer that receives public subsidies, or government-run liquor store monopolies found in many countries. Employees of these companies are foreign public officials under the Convention, even if building airplanes or selling alcohol may not be typical "public functions" in some countries.

Croatia's definition of a foreign public official is narrower than the Convention in this respect. The definition of an "official" in CA Art. 87(3) covers "typical" public functions such as those of state officials, civil servants, and judges. SOE employees are clearly omitted. The definition of a "responsible person" in CA Art. 87(6) covers SOE employees, since it includes "a natural person who manages the affairs of a legal person or is explicitly or actually entrusted with the performance of activities in the field of activity of a legal person". But as mentioned earlier, the definition of a "responsible person" may apply only to individuals in Croatia, not foreign countries. Some Croatian prosecutors and judges state that bribery of foreign SOEs is covered by the commercial bribery offence (CA Art. 253). But this offence raises additional problems, such as lower sanctions and proof of additional elements (such as damage). Coverage of foreign SOE employees has been the subject of recommendations by the OECD Working Group on Bribery.[4]

Officials and agents of a "public international organisation"

Convention Art. 1(4)(a) states that a "foreign public official" includes "any official or agent of a public international organisation". Commentary 17 elaborates that a "public international organisation" includes "any international organisation formed by states, governments, or other public international organisations, whatever the form of organisation and scope of competence, including, for example, a regional economic integration organisation such as the European Communities."

Croatia only meets this requirement partially. The definition of an "official" in CA Art. 87(3) refers to the European Union and an international organisation "of which the Republic of Croatia is a member". Similarly, the definition covers an international court or arbitration tribunal "whose jurisdiction the Republic of Croatia accepts". The Convention is not so limited, as the OECD Working Group on Bribery has observed.[5] Extending Croatia's definition is important since there are many international organisations of which it is not a member, e.g. regional multilateral development banks outside Europe. Otherwise, a Croatian individual could commit bribery on behalf of a company from a country that is a member of such an international organisation, for example.

Meaning of a "foreign country"

Convention Art. 1(1) prohibits the bribery of officials of "a foreign country". This term is very broadly interpreted. Art. 1(4)(b) stipulates that the term "foreign country" includes "all levels and subdivisions of government, from national to local". Commentary 18 adds that the concept "is not limited to states, but includes any organised foreign area or entity, such as an autonomous territory or a separate customs territory."

Croatia's definition of a foreign country includes at least some of the entities contemplated by the Convention. Read as a whole, CA Art. 87(3) defines an "official" to include public officials and civil servants of a "foreign state". It also covers "an official or clerk in a unit of local and regional self-government" in a foreign state. Croatian authorities at the fact-finding mission state that there is no requirement that Croatia officially recognises the foreign state in question. As mentioned many times above, the definition of a "responsible person" in CA Art. 87(6) does not refer to a "foreign state". Neither provision explicitly mentions further subdivisions, such as an organised foreign area or entity, autonomous territory or a separate customs territory. The OECD Working Group on Bribery has recommended that countries clarify the coverage of these sub-state entities.[6]

Autonomous definition of a foreign public official

Commentary 3 of the Convention states that the definition of a "foreign public official" must be "autonomous". Proof of the law of the country of the foreign public official should not be a strict necessity. The test is instead functional. In other words, a person is a foreign public official if he/she performs one of the functions described in Convention Art. 1(4)(a). The individual's status under the foreign country's law is not determinative. The OECD Working Group on Bribery has recommended on many occasions that countries adopt an autonomous definition of a "foreign public official".[7]

The Ministry of Justice and Public Administration asserts that Croatia's definition of a "foreign public official" is autonomous . It states that this is clear from the wording of CA Art. 87(3) which defines a public official using a "functional approach". A person is a foreign public official if he/she "performs duties corresponding to the duties of the persons who have status of official in the Republic of Croatia." It is "irrelevant whether a person has a status of an official under the law of foreign country or international organisation."

Practitioners at the fact-finding mission are less sure. Prosecutors state that they would seek evidence of a foreign public official's status under foreign law. Absent such proof, they are not sure that they could secure a conviction for foreign bribery. Judges state that, in a domestic bribery case, they would ask for documentary proof of the official's status. Transplanting the reasoning to a foreign bribery case, they expect that similar evidence would be obtained through mutual legal assistance. A defence lawyer at the fact-finding mission is more conclusive, stating that proof of the foreign public official's legal capacity is certainly required.

4.3.7. For that official or for a third party

Convention Art. 1(1) requires the coverage of bribes paid to an official "or for a third party". Croatia's CA Art. 294 covers such third-party beneficiaries by referring to bribes intended for an official "or another person".

4.3.8. In order that the official act or refrain from acting in relation to the performance of official duties

Convention Art. 1(1) covers bribery "in order that the official act or refrain from acting in relation to the performance of official duties". Croatia's foreign bribery offence clearly applies to such cases. CA Art. 294(1) covers bribery in order that an official act or omit to act when he/she should not. Art. 294(2) covers bribery to induce an official to act or omit to act when he/she should. In either case, it is an offence regardless of whether the official's act or omissions are "within or outside the limits of his/her authority".

However, the Convention goes further and requires coverage of bribery in exchange for an act beyond an official's competence. Art. 1(1) prohibits bribery "in order that an official act or refrain from acting "in relation to the performance of official duties". This phrase includes "any use of the public official's position, whether or not within the official's authorised competence", according to Art. 1(4)(c). Commentary 19 adds that this would cover a case where an executive of a company gives a bribe to a senior official of a government. The official then uses his/her office – though acting outside his/her competence – to make another official award a contract to the company.

Croatia prohibits such cases of bribery to act outside official competence. CA Art. 294 applies to an official's acts or omissions whether "within or outside the limits of his/her authority". However, the offence concerns acts and omissions that an official should or should not do. It does not deal with situations when there is no explicit requirement for an official to act or a prohibition from acting. The Ministry of Justice and Public Administration states that such a case is instead covered by the trading in influence offence in CA Art. 296. This provision prohibits the giving of a bribe to someone to use his/her "official or social position or influence to mediate" the act or omission of an official. The offence is subject to the same range of sanctions as active foreign bribery.

4.3.9. In order to obtain or retain business or other improper advantage in the conduct of international business

Croatia's foreign bribery offence in CA Art. 294 is not restricted to bribery in a business context. Convention Art. 1(1) prohibits the bribery of a foreign public official "to obtain or retain business or other improper advantage in the conduct of international business". CA Art. 294 does not have a similar limitation. In this respect, the offence is broader than Convention Art. 1(1).

Croatian authorities state that CA Art. 294 meets two further requirements of the Convention. It is an offence under the provision whether or not the briber is the best qualified bidder for a contract or can otherwise be awarded the business (Commentary 4). It is also an offence if the briber obtains something to which he/she is not clearly entitled, for example, an operating permit for a factory which fails to meet the statutory requirements (Commentary 5). Supporting case law or jurisprudence is not provided, however. The application of these requirements to legal persons is considered in Section 5.5.

4.4. Complicity to commit foreign bribery

Convention Art. 1(2) states that "each Party shall take any measures necessary to establish that complicity in, including incitement, aiding and abetting, or authorisation of an act of bribery of a foreign public official shall be a criminal offence." Commentary 11 clarifies that these offences "are understood in terms of their normal content in national legal systems. Accordingly, if authorisation, incitement, or one of the other listed acts, which does not lead to further action, is not itself punishable under a Party's legal system, then the Party would not be required to make it punishable with respect to bribery of a foreign public official."

Croatia addresses complicity in the general part of the Criminal Act. As mentioned in Section 4.3.5, CA Art. 36 provides that a person who commits an offence "through another person" is liable as a principal. Liability as co-perpetrators arises if several persons commit an offence based on a joint decision, and each participates or significantly contributes to the commission of the offence. The Ministry of Justice and Public Administration states that this provision also covers authorisation to commit an offence. In addition, under CA Art. 37(1) a person who intentionally incites another to commit an offence is punishable as if he/she had committed it. A person who intentionally assists another to commit an offence is liable under CA Art. 38, but may be punished "more leniently" than the perpetrator.

4.5. Attempt and conspiracy to commit foreign bribery

Convention Art. 1(2) states that "attempt and conspiracy to bribe a foreign public official shall be criminal offences to the same extent as attempt and conspiracy to bribe a public official."

In Croatia, the crime of attempt applies equally to foreign and domestic bribery. Under CA Art. 34, a person is guilty of attempt if he/she intends to commit an offence, and undertakes an action that "spatially and temporally immediately precedes" the commission of the offence. A person who attempts an offence may be punished "less severely" than a perpetrator who carries out the act. The provision applies only when explicitly prescribed by law or when the offence that is attempted is punishable by imprisonment of at least five years. Attempt therefore applies to foreign (and domestic) bribery to breach duties, which is punishable by one to eight years' imprisonment (CA Art. 294(1)). Attempt also applies to foreign (and domestic) bribery to perform duties, since the maximum penalty for the offence is five years' imprisonment (CA Art. 294(2)).

Conspiracy to commit foreign bribery also applies to the same extent as domestic bribery. Under CA Art. 327, it is a crime to agree with someone to commit an offence that is punishable by imprisonment of more than three years. The active foreign and domestic bribery offences qualify for this provision. A conspiracy is punishable by imprisonment of up to three years.

4.6. Defences to foreign bribery

4.6.1. Defence of small facilitation payments

The Convention does not require Parties to criminalise small facilitation payments. Commentary 9 defines such payments as those "made to induce public officials to perform their functions, such as issuing licenses or permits". These payments are not considered as made "to obtain or retain business or other improper advantage". They are therefore not prohibited by the Convention. However, in view of the corrosive effect of this phenomenon, the 2009 Anti-Bribery Recommendation VI asks countries to periodically review their policies and approach on small facilitation payments, to combat the phenomenon, and encourage companies to prohibit or discourage the use of small facilitation payments in their internal controls, ethics and compliance programmes.

Croatian authorities state that their foreign bribery offence prohibits "small facilitation payments". CA Art. 87(24) defines a bribe as any undue reward, gift or benefit "regardless of value". This overrides a defence of an "insignificant crime" in CA Art. 33. This latter provision states that there is no criminal offence if "the degree of guilt of the perpetrator is low, the offence had no consequences or the consequences are insignificant, and there is no need to punish the perpetrator." The Ministry of Justice and Public Administration states that CA Art. 33 is not applied in practice in corruption cases. Data on the provision's application are not available.

4.6.2. Effective regret

CA Art. 294(3) sets out "effective regret" to foreign (and domestic) bribery. A briber may be "released from punishment" if he/she pays a bribe in response to the official's request. He/she must also report the crime either before its discovery, or before learning of its discovery. The offender escapes punishment but is nevertheless prosecuted and a conviction is entered, as a prosecutor at the fact-finding mission points out. CA Art. 50(2) further provides that the briber may receive more lenient sanctions in lieu of a full release from punishment. Croatian authorities state that the policy reason for the provision is to encourage the reporting of bribery. Some prosecutors and judges add that liability would be excluded only if an individual was coerced by an official to pay a bribe. This requirement is not stipulated in the provision, however. Statistics provided by Croatian authorities indicate that this provision has only been used once in 2015-2019. A similar provision applies to legal persons (see Section 5.8).

A key feature of the provision is that it is discretionary and that it does not preclude confiscation of the proceeds of bribery. Fact-finding mission participants state that it is for a judge to decide whether the briber should be released from punishment. In making this decision, the court would consider factors such as the circumstances and impact of the offence, and the personal circumstances of the offender. One judge states that she would not apply the provision if the offence is discovered before the briber's report. Another judge states that the briber is found guilty and only released from punishment. Confiscation can therefore be imposed, since CA Art. 5 states that "no one may retain the proceeds of an illegal act".

4.6.3. Defence of necessity

Commentary 7 states that foreign bribery is an offence irrespective of, *inter alia*, the alleged necessity of the payment in order to obtain or retain business or other improper advantage.

Croatia's defence of necessity does not apply to foreign bribery. CA Art. 21(2) limits the defence to situations where the commission of an offence is necessary to "repel a simultaneous or imminent unlawful attack from oneself or another". The provision therefore does not apply to bribery to obtain or retain business or other advantage.

4.7. Conclusions on Croatia's foreign bribery offence

Croatia's foreign bribery offence in CA Art. 294 contains many of the essential features required by the OECD Anti-Bribery Convention. The offence broadly applies to any natural person. It explicitly covers the modalities of an offer, promise and giving of a bribe. Bribes can be any undue reward, gift or other property or non-property benefit, regardless of value. Bribes paid to third party beneficiaries are expressly covered. Bribery through intermediaries is covered through the CA provisions on co-perpetration. The trading in influence offence in CA Art. 296 covers some forms of bribery in order that an official act outside official competence. General provisions in the CA provide for complicity and attempted foreign bribery.

To further strengthen its foreign bribery offence, Croatia could consider the following:

a   Take steps to ensure that the offence's intent requirement is sufficiently broad to cover typical foreign bribery transactions, in particular bribery committed through intermediaries

b   Expand the definition of a foreign public official, including to persons who hold legislative office in or who exercise a public function for a foreign country; employees of foreign state-owned or controlled enterprises; and officials of all public international organisations, including those in which Croatia is not a member

c   Ensure that the definition of a foreign public official is autonomous and does not require proof of foreign law

d   Clarify that the definition of a foreign country includes "all levels and subdivisions of government, from national to local", as well as any organised foreign area or entity, such as an autonomous territory or a separate customs territory.

References

OECD (2020), *Costa Rica Phase 2 Report*, https://www.oecd.org/corruption/Costa Rica-Phase-2-Report-ENG.pdf#page=52&zoom=100,82,214. [7]

OECD (2020), *Foreign bribery and the role of intermediaries, managers and gender*, https://www.oecd.org/corruption/Foreign-bribery-and-the-role-of-intermediaries-managers-and-gender.pdf. [2]

OECD (2020), *Iceland Phase 4 Report*, https://www.oecd.org/daf/anti-bribery/Iceland-Phase-4-Report-ENG.pdf#page=23&zoom=100,82,569. [10]

OECD (2019), *Latvia Phase 3 Report*, https://www.oecd.org/corruption/anti-bribery/OECD-Latvia-Phase-3-Report-ENG.pdf#page=16&zoom=100,82,457. [6]

OECD (2017), *Argentina Phase 3bis Report*, http://www.oecd.org/corruption/anti-bribery/Argentina-Phase-3bis-Report-ENG.pdf#page=15&zoom=100,76,633. [21]

OECD (2017), *Finland Phase 4 Report*, https://www.oecd.org/corruption/anti-bribery/Finland-Phase-4-Report-ENG.pdf#page=30&zoom=100,82,662. [5]

OECD (2015), *Greece Phase 3bis Report*, http://www.oecd.org/daf/anti-bribery/Greece-Phase-3bis-Report-EN.pdf#page=16&zoom=100,76,133. [12]

OECD (2015), *Phase 2 Report on Implementing the OECD Anti-Bribery Convention in Latvia*, https://www.oecd.org/daf/anti-bribery/Latvia-Phase-2-Report-ENG.pdf#page=54&zoom=100,76,165. [4]

OECD (2014), *Argentina Phase 3 Report*, https://www.oecd.org/daf/anti-bribery/Argentina-Phase-3-Report-ENG.pdf#page=14&zoom=100,82,200. [20]

OECD (2014), *Slovenia Phase 3 Report*, http://www.oecd.org/daf/anti-bribery/SloveniaPhase3ReportEN.pdf#page=12&zoom=100,82,550. [8]

OECD (2013), *Portugal Phase 3 Report*, https://www.oecd.org/daf/anti-bribery/Portugalphase3reportEN.pdf. [16]

OECD (2012), *Slovak Republic Phase 3 Report*, https://www.oecd.org/daf/anti-bribery/SlovakRepublicphase3reportEN.pdf#page=12&zoom=100,76,361. [14]

OECD (2012), *Spain Phase 3 Report*, https://www.oecd.org/daf/anti-bribery/Spainphase3reportEN.pdf#page=14&zoom=100,76,550. [19]

OECD (2010), *Iceland Phase 3 Report*, https://www.oecd.org/daf/anti-bribery/anti-briberyconvention/Icelandphase3reportEN.pdf#page=10&zoom=100,82,550. [9]

OECD (2009), *Typologies on the Role of Intermediaries in International Business Transactions*, https://www.oecd.org/daf/anti-bribery/anti-briberyconvention/43879503.pdf. [3]

OECD (2007), *Portugal Phase 2 Report*, https://www.oecd.org/daf/anti-bribery/anti-briberyconvention/38320110.pdf#page=44&zoom=100,82,250. [15]

OECD (2005), *Belgium Phase 2 Report*, https://www.oecd.org/daf/anti-bribery/anti-briberyconvention/35461651.pdf#page=35&zoom=100,82,700. [17]

OECD (2005), *Slovak Republic Phase 2*, https://www.oecd.org/daf/anti-bribery/anti-briberyconvention/35778308.pdf#page=30&zoom=100,76,433. [13]

OECD (2005), *Sweden Phase 2 Report*, https://www.oecd.org/daf/anti-bribery/anti-briberyconvention/35394676.pdf#page=37&zoom=100,82,550. [11]

OECD (2004), *Mexico Phase 2 Report*, https://www.oecd.org/daf/anti-bribery/anti-briberyconvention/33746033.pdf#page=11&zoom=100,82,500. [18]

OECD (n.d.), *Country monitoring of the OECD Anti-Bribery Convention*, https://www.oecd.org/daf/anti-bribery/countrymonitoringoftheoecdanti-briberyconvention.htm. [1]

Notes

[1] Criminal Act (*Kazneni zakon*), Official Gazette No. 125/11, 144/12, 56/15, 61/15, 101/17, 118/18, 126/19, 84/21.

[2] For example, see (OECD, 2015[4]), paras. 194-197 and Recommendation 13(a); (OECD, 2017[5]), paras. 80-83 and Recommendation 3; (OECD, 2019[6]), para. 31 and Recommendation 1(a); (OECD, 2020[7]), paras. 197-201 and Recommendation 12(a).

[3] Act on Obligations and Rights of State Officials (*Zakon o obvezama i pravima državnih dužnosnika*), Official Gazette No. 101/98, 135/98, 105/99, 25/00, 73/00, 30/01, 59/01, 114/01, 153/02, 163/03, 16/04, 30/04, 121/05, 151/05, 141/06, 17/07, 34/07, 107/07, 60/08, 38/09, 150/11, 22/13, 102/14, 103/14, 03/15, 93/16, 44/17, 66/19.

[4] For example, see (OECD, 2014[8]), para. 26 and Recommendation 1(b); (OECD, 2010[9]), paras. 13-17 and Recommendation 1; (OECD, 2020[10]), paras. 60-67 and Recommendation 5.

[5] For example, see (OECD, 2005[11]), paras. 144-153 and 227; (OECD, 2015[12]), para. 40 and Recommendation 2(c); (OECD, 2005[13]), paras. 135-141; (OECD, 2012[14]), paras. 22-24 and Recommendation 1(b).

[6] For example, see (OECD, 2007[15]), para. 134; (OECD, 2013[16]), para. 36 and Recommendation 1(b); (OECD, 2014[8]), para. 21 and Recommendation 1(a).

[7] For example, see (OECD, 2005[17]), paras. 118-122 and 178(k); (OECD, 2004[18]), paras. 34-35 and 185(b); (OECD, 2012[19]), paras. 24-26 and Recommendation 2(a); (OECD, 2014[20]), para. 34 and Recommendation 1(a); (OECD, 2017[21]), paras. 43-44 and Recommendation 1(a).

5 Liability of legal persons for foreign bribery

This chapter analyses the main elements of Croatia's Act on the Responsibility of Legal Persons for Criminal Offences to determine whether these are in line with the OECD standards for establishing the liability of legal persons for the bribery of a foreign public official.

The liability of legal persons is the second criterion for acceding to the Anti-Bribery Convention that is related to legal and enforcement framework for fighting foreign bribery. The OECD Working Group on Bribery assesses an accession candidate's corporate liability framework against Convention Article 2 and 2009 Recommendation Annex I.

5.1. OECD standards on corporate liability

Art. 2 of the Convention requires countries to create the liability of legal persons for foreign bribery:

> *Article 2*
>
> *Responsibility of Legal Persons*
>
> *Each Party shall take such measures as may be necessary, in accordance with its legal principles, to establish the liability of legal persons for the bribery of a foreign public official.*

Additional guidance is in Commentary 20 of the Convention, and Annex I.B and I.C of the 2009 Anti-Bribery Recommendation.

5.2. Croatia's corporate liability framework

In Croatia, corporate liability for criminal offences is set out in the Act on the Responsibility of Legal Persons for Criminal Offences (Corporate Liability Law, CLL). The CLL was enacted in 2003 and last amended in 2012.[1] It establishes criminal responsibility of legal entities for any criminal offence – including foreign bribery – under Croatian law (CLL Art. 3(2)).

The CLL determines the preconditions of liability, sanctions and confiscation, as well as criminal procedure rules for legal entities (CLL Art. 1(1)). Unless the CLL prescribes otherwise, the provisions of the Criminal Act, the Criminal Procedure Act and the Law on the Office for the Prevention of Corruption and Organised Crime apply to legal entities (CLL Art. 2).

5.3. Legal entities subject to liability, including successor liability

Any entity that possesses legal personality under Croatian law can be found liable under the CLL. In addition, CLL Art. 1(2) explicitly applies the CLL to foreign entities that are considered as legal persons under Croatian law. The only exceptions are the Republic of Croatia, and units of local and regional self-government when acting in the exercise of their public authority (CLL Art. 6). The CLL also covers state-owned and/or controlled enterprises, according to Croatian authorities. However, in 2015-2019 USKOK did not investigate any state-owned and/or controlled enterprises. Croatian authorities were also unable to provide an example of past prosecutions against such enterprises.

CLL Art. 7 provides for successor liability. If a legal person ceases to exist "before the criminal proceedings have ended" or "after the final completion of the criminal proceedings", then sanctions or other measures can be imposed on the entity's "general legal successor". Croatian authorities explain that the "general legal successor" is an entity resulting from forms of corporate reorganisation governed by Croatia's Companies Act and other legislation on legal persons.[2] CLL Art. 7 further provides that legal persons subject to bankruptcy proceedings shall be punished for criminal offences committed both before and during such proceedings.

5.4. Level of authority of the natural person whose acts lead to corporate liability

The Anti-Bribery Convention requires countries to ensure that legal persons are held liable for foreign bribery committed by not only senior corporate officers but also lower-level employees. The 2009 Anti-Bribery Recommendation Annex I.B therefore requires systems for the liability of legal persons to take one of the following alternative approaches:

a   the level of authority of the person whose conduct triggers the liability of the legal person is flexible and reflects the wide variety of decision-making systems in legal persons; or

b   the approach is functionally equivalent to the foregoing even though it is only triggered by acts of persons with the highest level managerial authority, because the following cases are covered:

   i.   A person with the highest level managerial authority offers, promises or gives a bribe to a foreign public official;

   ii. A person with the highest level managerial authority directs or authorises a lower level person to offer, promise or give a bribe to a foreign public official; and

   iii. A person with the highest level managerial authority fails to prevent a lower level person from bribing a foreign public official, including through a failure to supervise him or her or through a failure to implement adequate internal controls, ethics and compliance programmes or measures.

In Croatia, corporate liability is triggered by the acts of "a responsible person" of the legal person, according to CLL Art. 3:

> *Article 3*
>
> *(1) A legal person shall be punished for the criminal offence of a responsible person if it violates a duty of a legal person or with which the legal person has achieved or should have achieved an illegal property gain for itself or another.*
>
> *(2) Under the conditions referred to in paragraph 1 of this Article, a legal person shall be punished for criminal offences prescribed by the Criminal Act and other laws in which criminal offences are prescribed.*

A "responsible person" is defined in CLL Art. 4:

> *Article 4*
>
> *The responsible person in the sense of this Act is a natural person who manages the affairs of a legal person or is entrusted with the performance of activities in the field of activity of a legal person.*

Foreign bribery committed by a senior corporate officer may thus result in corporate liability under the CLL. The definition of a "responsible person" includes "a natural person who manages the affairs of a legal person". This should cover a "person with the highest level managerial authority" within the meaning of 2009 Anti-Bribery Recommendation. As explained in Section 4.4, a senior corporate officer who authorises or directs a lower-level person to bribe a foreign public official is guilty of complicity or incitement under CA Art. 36 or 37.

The CLL also provides corporate liability for foreign bribery committed by a lower-level person in the company. A "responsible person" includes someone who is "is entrusted with the performance of activities in the field of activity of a legal person". The definition does not take into account the seniority of the person in question. During the fact-finding mission, one prosecutor states that a low-ranking individual can be a responsible person "as long as he/she is linked to the activity of the legal person". A second prosecutor refers to an actual case in which a worker at a warehouse met the definition. An academic agrees that low level employees are covered.

The Ministry of Justice and Public Administration describes a different theory of corporate liability for bribery committed by a lower-level person. Liability arises if the crime was committed as a result of company management's failure to supervise the lower-level employee. Company management, as a "responsible person" who manages the affairs of the legal person under CLL Art. 4, thereby fails to perform its duties which results in an offence of abuse of office and authority under CA Art. 291.[3] However, this offence requires proof that failure to perform duties results in an advantage or damage to another person.

5.5. Standard of liability

The Convention Art. 1 covers bribery "in order to obtain or retain business or other improper advantage." Commentaries 4 and 5 clarify that this should constitute an offence whether or not the company concerned was the best qualified bidder for a contract or could otherwise have been awarded the business. They also explain that "other improper advantage" refers to something to which the company concerned was not clearly entitled, such as an operating permit for a factory which fails to meet the statutory requirements.

Under CLL Art. 3(1), not all criminal offences committed by a "responsible person" result in corporate liability. Instead, the legal person's responsibility is triggered only if (i) the offence violates a "duty of the legal person"; or (ii) the crime has or should have achieved an "illegal property gain" for the legal person or a third person. These conditions are not cumulative.

Bribery generally would not lead to liability under the first branch of Art. 3(1), i.e. as a violation of a "duty of the legal person". A prosecutor during the fact-finding mission states plainly that bribery, in and of itself, does not amount to a breach of a "duty of a legal person" under Croatian law. Instead, such duties relate to the reason for which the legal person was established, according to the Ministry of Justice and Public Administration. For example, if a legal person was created with a goal of protecting the environment, then an act causing environmental damage would be a breach of a "duty of the legal person". A Croatian lawyer and an academic take a similar view, stating that the "duties of a legal person" are found in the legal person's documents of incorporation deposited at the corporate registry. The academic adds that there could be additional duties such as to undergo audit or conduct due diligence on business and human rights. A prosecutor also suggests in passing that evading taxes and accounting misconduct might amount to breaches of duties. But no discussant considers that bribery necessarily amounts to a breach of a "duty of a legal person".

Some acts of bribery might also not trigger corporate liability under the second branch of CLL Art. 3(1), i.e. where the offence has or should have achieved an "illegal property gain". All participants at the fact-finding mission explain that an "illegal property gain" equates to "property gain from a criminal offence" defined in CA Art. 87(22). This means that a contract or job opportunity obtained through bribery is not a property but non-property gain, according to two prosecutors. A lawyer adds that a property gain is something that is capable of being expressed in money. Hence, bribery to avoid a safety inspection is a "property gain" only if there is proof that a fine has been avoided.

The *INA/MOL* case vividly illustrates the obstacle posed by the need of an "illegal property gain" for corporate liability. The case involves allegations that a company CEO bribed a former Prime Minister to obtain a stake and board seats in a Croatian state-owned enterprise. Prosecutors at the fact-finding mission elaborate that the purpose of the crime was to acquire controlling shares in the Croatian state-owned enterprise. The bribery thus only "enabled business". It did not produce any wrongful proceeds or "illegal property gain" under CLL Art. 3 that would be necessary to impose liability against the company.

Restricting corporate liability to bribery that produces an "illegal property gain" does not meet the requirements of the Convention. Parties to the Convention must impose liability against legal persons for foreign bribery, which is defined in Art. 1 as bribery to "to obtain or retain business or other improper advantage". This term is interpreted broadly. Non-property gains such as an operating permit for a factory must be covered, as indicated in Commentary 5. The Working Group has stated that liability should also arise when bribery results in a "property loss": companies may win an unprofitable contract merely to gain market entry.[4] The Working Group has therefore criticised limiting liability to bribery that "was aimed at or has resulted in the legal entity gaining financial advantage." Such a requirement causes "potential difficulties arising from the necessity to prove an intended or actual financial advantage or profit".[5]

Given this broad interpretation, the foreign bribery offences of Parties to the Convention thus cover bribery to obtain a wide range advantages. Examples include the processing of official documents, such as visas or work permits; the provision of services normally offered to the public, such as mail pick-up and delivery, telecommunication services, power and water supply, police protection, loading and unloading of cargo, protection of perishable products from deterioration, or the scheduling of inspections related to contract performance or transit of goods; a right of entry into a country; exemption from compliance with regulatory operating conditions; and obtaining the delivery of supplies or false records.[6]

That Croatia's regime falls below the Convention's standards can also be seen from its differential treatment of natural and legal person liability for foreign bribery. Art. 2 of the Convention requires corporate liability for all acts of foreign bribery committed by natural persons as defined in Art. 1. That is not the case in Croatia, where foreign bribery that produces a non-property gain leads to liability for natural but not legal persons.

5.6. Bribes paid through intermediaries, including related legal persons

Annex I.C of the 2009 Anti-Bribery Recommendation prescribes that the Parties to the Anti-Bribery Convention should ensure that "a legal person cannot avoid responsibility by using intermediaries, including related legal persons, to offer, promise or give a bribe to a foreign public official on its behalf."

Croatian authorities state that legal persons can be liable for using an intermediary such as an agent or contractor to bribe foreign public officials. A person in a company who uses an intermediary to commit foreign bribery is liable for the offence as a principal or co-perpetrator (see Section 4.3.5). If the person who uses the intermediary is also a "responsible person" in the company (see Section 5.4) then the company is also liable for the offence, assuming other requirements in the CLL are met. A prosecutor in the fact-finding mission states that the legal person in this scenario would be liable, even if the intermediary used to commit bribery is not a full-time employee of the company.

The CLL does not provide special rules on corporate liability for bribery committed through a related legal person. The Ministry of Justice and Public Administration states that a parent company would be liable if the CLL requirements are met. This occurs for example, if a "responsible person" of the parent company is guilty of directing or authorising the subsidiary to commit foreign bribery. A prosecutor adds that this would occur only if the individual in the parent company is responsible for overseeing the subsidiary. The bribery would also have to benefit the parent or the corporate group.

5.7. Proceedings against legal persons

The 2009 Anti-Bribery Recommendation Annex I.B states that a country's system of liability of legal persons "should not restrict the liability to cases where the natural person or persons who perpetrated the offence are prosecuted or convicted."

The CLL meets this requirement. Art. 5(1) states that "the liability of a legal person shall be based on the fault of the responsible person." Art. 5(2) adds that "A legal person shall also be punished for the criminal offence of a responsible person even in the case when the existence of legal or actual obstacles to determining the responsibility of the responsible person is established". Croatian authorities explain that examples of "legal obstacles" include immunity and amnesty. "Actual obstacles" include the impossibility of identifying the natural person; the natural person's death or incapacity to stand trial; and if the natural person has absconded or is abroad.

5.8. Effective regret

The principle of effective regret applies to natural persons (see Section 4.6.2) as well as legal persons. Under CLL Art. 12a, "a legal person who reported the criminal offence of a responsible person before its discovery or before learning that the offence has been discovered, may be released from punishment." As with natural persons, Croatian authorities state that the purpose of this provision is to encourage the reporting of crimes. This release from punishment is a discretionary decision of the court ("*may* be released from punishment"). However, the CLL does not have a provision equivalent to CA Art. 50(2) that allows a court to impose a more lenient punishment as an alternative to release from punishment. Croatia does not have statistics on the application of CLL Art. 12a. Prosecutors at the fact-finding mission are not aware of a case in which CLL Art. 12a was applied. They explain that the provision could apply to a large company whose management discovers and reports offences committed by previous management.

5.9. Conclusions on liability of legal persons for foreign bribery in Croatia

Croatia's CLL provides for the liability of legal persons for foreign bribery and meets many of the standards demanded by the OECD Anti-Bribery Convention. The CLL broadly applies to any entity that possesses legal personality, and expressly covers foreign entities that are considered as legal persons under Croatian law. Liability can result from bribery committed by senior corporate officers, lower-level employees, and intermediaries (including related legal persons). The prosecution or conviction of a natural person is not a prerequisite to corporate liability.

To further strengthen its foreign bribery offence, Croatia could consider taking steps to ensure that liability can result from all acts of foreign bribery, and not only those that result in an "illegal property gain" to the legal person.

References

Council of Europe Group of States against Corruption, C. (2005), *Second Evaluation Round Report*, https://rm.coe.int/CoERMPublicCommonSearchServices/DisplayDCTMContent?documentId=09000016806c2d1c. [1]

OECD (2011), *Luxembourg Phase 3 Report*, https://www.oecd.org/daf/anti-bribery/anti-briberyconvention/Luxembourgphase3reportEN.pdf. [6]

OECD (2005), *Hungary Phase 2 Report*, https://www.oecd.org/daf/anti-bribery/anti-briberyconvention/34918600.pdf. [7]

OECD (2002), *New Zealand Phase 1 Report*, https://www.oecd.org/daf/anti-bribery/anti-briberyconvention/2088257.pdf. [5]

OECD (1999), *Canada Phase 1 Report*, https://www.oecd.org/daf/anti-bribery/anti-briberyconvention/2385703.pdf. [2]

OECD (1999), *Chile Phase 1 Report*, https://www.oecd.org/daf/anti-bribery/anti-briberyconvention/33742154.pdf. [3]

OECD (1999), *Greece Phase 1 Report*, https://www.oecd.org/daf/anti-bribery/anti-briberyconvention/2386792.pdf. [4]

Notes

[1] Act on the Responsibility of Legal Persons for Criminal Offences (*Zakon o odgovornosti pravnih osoba za kaznena djela*), Official Gazette No. 151/03, 110/07, 45/11, 143/12.

[2] See e.g. Companies Act (*Zakon o trgovačkim društvima*), Official Gazette No. 111/93, 34/99, 121/99, 52/00, 118/03, 107/07, 146/08, 137/09, 125/11, 152/11, 111/12, 68/13, 110/15, 40/19, Arts. 512 and 550a(6).

[3] In another evaluation, Croatia also asserted that in these cases company management can be liable for the offence under CA/1997 Art. 339 for a negligent failure to perform supervisory duties resulting in a violation of the rights of third parties or considerable property damage. (Council of Europe Group of States against Corruption, 2005[1]), para. 65.

[4] (OECD, 2011[6]), para. 44.

[5] (OECD, 2005[7]), paras. 147-149 and 210(a).

[6] (OECD, 1999[2]), p. 6; (OECD, 1999[3]), p. 7; (OECD, 1999[4]), p. 5; (OECD, 2002[5]), p. 8.

6 Sanctions for foreign bribery

This chapter examines whether Croatia is able to impose "effective, proportionate and dissuasive" sanctions against natural and legal persons for foreign bribery, as well as to confiscate the bribe and the proceeds of bribery as required by the OECD Anti-Bribery Convention.

The third Accession Criterion on the framework for fighting foreign bribery concerns the sanctions for this crime. The OECD Working Group on Bribery assesses the sanctions available in an accession candidate against Convention Art. 3. It also considers the sanctions that have been imposed in practice for foreign and domestic bribery.

6.1. OECD standards on sanctions for foreign bribery

Convention Art. 3 deals with sanctions for foreign bribery. In sum, countries must be able to impose "effective, proportionate and dissuasive" sanctions against natural and legal persons for this crime. They must also confiscate the bribe and the proceeds of foreign bribery, and consider additional civil or administrative sanctions:

> *Article 3*
>
> *Sanctions*
>
> *The bribery of a foreign public official shall be punishable by effective, proportionate and dissuasive criminal penalties. The range of penalties shall be comparable to that applicable to the bribery of the Party's own public officials and shall, in the case of natural persons, include deprivation of liberty sufficient to enable effective mutual legal assistance and extradition.*
>
> *In the event that, under the legal system of a Party, criminal responsibility is not applicable to legal persons, that Party shall ensure that legal persons shall be subject to effective, proportionate and dissuasive non-criminal sanctions, including monetary sanctions, for bribery of foreign public officials.*
>
> *Each Party shall take such measures as may be necessary to provide that the bribe and the proceeds of the bribery of a foreign public official, or property the value of which corresponds to that of such proceeds, are subject to seizure and confiscation or that monetary sanctions of comparable effect are applicable.*
>
> *Each Party shall consider the imposition of additional civil or administrative sanctions upon a person subject to sanctions for the bribery of a foreign public official.*

6.2. Principal penalties for bribery of a domestic and foreign public official

6.2.1. Sanctions against natural persons for domestic and foreign bribery

Sanctions available against natural persons

Foreign and domestic bribery are punishable under CA Art. 294 by imprisonment of one to eight years for bribery in breach of duty, and six months to five years for bribery to perform one's duty. CA Art. 47 provides for aggravating and mitigating factors for sentencing. The court must consider all relevant circumstances, and especially the degree of endangerment or violation of a legally protected good; motive for committing the crime; degree of violation of the perpetrator's duties; manner of the offence's commission and consequences of the crime; the perpetrator's personal and financial circumstances, and behaviour after the crime; the relationship with the victim and the efforts to compensate the damage.

Fines are also available. Under CA Art. 40(4), a fine can be imposed as a principal penalty for offences that carry a sentence of imprisonment of up to three years. Foreign and domestic bribery do not qualify because their maximum sentences exceed this threshold. However, a fine can be imposed as an ancillary penalty under CA Art. 40(2) and (5) for "offences committed out of greed." Croatian authorities state that foreign and domestic bribery are always motivated by greed.

The quantum of fines is set out in CA Art. 42. A fine for offences committed out of greed is between 30 and 500 "daily units". The number of daily units is determined based on the aggravating and mitigating sentencing factors in CA Art. 47. The monetary amount of each "daily unit" is then fixed according to the perpetrator's income, property, and average expenses necessary for maintaining him/herself and his/her family. The amount of a "daily unit" must be between HRK 20 and HRK 10 000, however. The available fine for foreign and domestic bribery is therefore HRK 600-5 million (EUR 80-660 000).

The maximum available fine might be considered insufficient. By definition, the Convention covers foreign bribery committed to obtain or retain international business. Many actual cases under the Convention have involved foreign bribery to win business and secure profits worth millions of euros. Substantial fines at least of the same order of magnitude is necessary as a deterrent. The Croatian Ministry of Justice and Public Administration argues that the amount of the fine must diminish the offender's standard of life while still allowing him/her (and his/her family) to live. However, dozens of individuals in the Croatian business community reportedly have hundreds of millions of euros in wealth. The maximum must by definition be capable of addressing such extreme cases. The Ministry also argues that confiscation is available (see Section 6.3.2). But the measure only removes ill-gotten gains. It puts the offender in the same position as before the crime, and is therefore not a sufficient deterrent for wrongdoing. The OECD Working Group on Bribery has therefore recommended that countries increase the maximum fines available against natural persons for foreign bribery, notwithstanding the availability of incarceration for the crime.[1]

A sentence may also be converted into community service (CA Art. 55) or suspended (CA Arts. 56-58). An imprisonment sentence of less than one year and a fine of less than 360 daily units can be converted into community service. An imprisonment sentence of not more than one year or a fine can be suspended and replaced with probation for one to five years. A fine or imprisonment of more than one and less than three years can also be suspended partially and served through probation. In deciding whether to suspend a sentence, the court considers factors such as the circumstances of the offence, and the offender's personality, antecedents, family circumstances, criminal history, post-offence behaviour, and likelihood of re-offending.

Sanctions against natural persons in practice

As explained in Section 7.3, there are no convictions in Croatia for foreign bribery. Croatia provided data on sanctions imposed for active domestic bribery under CA Art. 294. The cases initiated under this provision between 2014 and 2019 have yielded 149 convictions, of which 124 (or 83%) resulted from non-trial resolutions.[2] Three convictions resulted in imprisonment sentences of over a year (one year and three months, two years, and two years and ten months). All but three of the remaining convictions resulted in jail of five months to one year. However, only seven prison sentences (5%) were served in custody. Most were suspended and replaced with probation (63%) or community service (32%). One offender was exempted from punishment due to effective regret (see Section 4.6.2). Fines were imposed against only five individuals (3%). Data on the amount of the fines are not available.

Figure 6.1. Sanctions against natural persons for domestic bribery (2015-19)

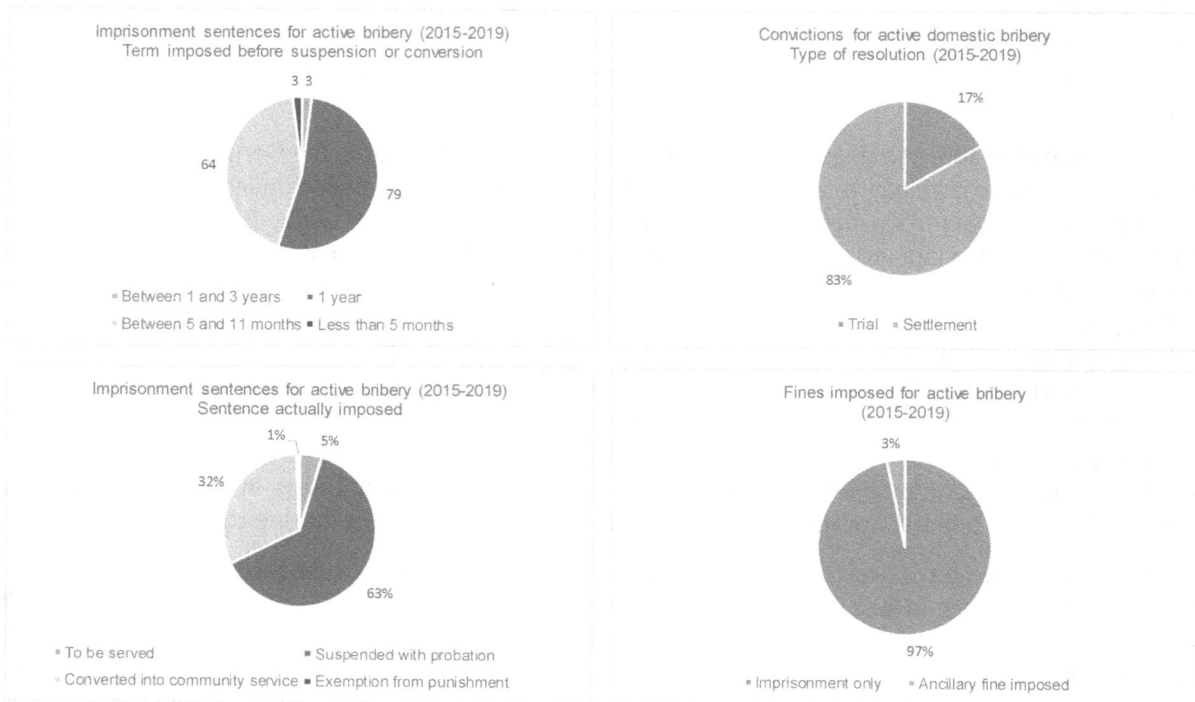

Source: USKOK

Croatian authorities provided additional information on the sanctions imposed in two high-level domestic corruption cases.[3] The sanctions imposed in these cases for the "active" side of corruption are also relatively low. Ancillary fines were also not imposed:

- In the *Planinska case*, a former parliamentarian and his companies paid the then-Prime Minister HRK 17 million (EUR 2.2 million) to sell a building to the government at a significantly inflated price. The defendants were convicted of abuse of office and authority and complicity in such offence (CA Arts. 291(2), 37 and 38). The former Prime Minister was sentenced to 6 years in prison. However, the former parliamentarian received a 1-year sentence that was replaced by community service.[4]

- In the *INA/MOL case*, a company CEO allegedly promised the then-Prime Minister EUR 10 million to acquire a substantial stake in a Croatian state-owned company and to divest unprofitable business. The CEO and former Prime Minister received 2 and 6 years in prison respectively. The charges were under the former Criminal Act, which only had a maximum sentence of 3 years for active bribery. The Supreme Court upheld the convictions in October 2021, but the defendants could still challenge these before Croatia's Constitutional Court.[5]

The OECD Working Group on Bribery often recommends that countries ensure that sanctions imposed in practice in foreign bribery cases are effective, proportionate and dissuasive. It has expressed concerns when, for instance, custodial sentences are rare in practice and most convictions result in conditional prison sentences and probation.[6]

6.2.2. Sanctions against legal persons for domestic and foreign bribery

Sanctions available against legal persons

CLL Art. 10 sets out the fines applicable for legal persons. Four ranges of fines are available depending on the punishment applicable to the natural person for the offence. CLL Art. 10(2) applies to offences punishable by imprisonment of five years or more but less than ten years, which is the case for foreign and domestic bribery. Legal persons are thus subject to a fine of HRK 15 000 to 10 million (EUR 2 000-1.3 million). If a legal person is convicted of two or more concurrent offences, the resulting fines cannot exceed the sum of the individual fines or the maximum legal measure of the fine (CLL Art. 11).

The maximum fines available against legal persons for foreign bribery are not effective, proportionate and dissuasive. As explained in the section on Sanctions available against natural persons, many cases under the Convention have involved companies committing foreign bribery to secure profits worth millions of euros. The maximum fine available in Croatia is well below these levels. The Croatian Ministry of Justice and Public Administration argues that confiscation is also available and important. However, confiscation is not a sufficient deterrent for wrongdoing, as pointed out in the section on Sanctions available against natural persons. The OECD Working Group on Bribery has recommended that countries increase the maximum fines available against legal persons for foreign bribery, regardless of the availability of additional administrative sanctions such as debarment and termination.[7]

Sentences against legal persons may be suspended (CLL Art. 13). A fine of less than HRK 50 000 (EUR 6 600) may be suspended for one to three years. The fine is cancelled if the legal person does not commit an offence during this period.

Termination of a legal person and additional administrative sanctions are considered in Section 6.5.

Sanctions against legal persons in practice

As explained in Section 7.3.3, in 2015-2019 Croatia has not investigated – and hence not sanctioned – legal persons for active foreign or domestic bribery. However, sanctions were imposed against 15 legal persons for other offences within the competence of the Office for the Suppression of Corruption and Organised Crime (USKOK). Nine of the convictions resulted from non-trial resolutions. Six of the legal persons were convicted of abuse of office and authority (CA Art. 291).[8] Leaving aside one fine that was exceptionally high (EUR 1.7 million), the average fine imposed for this offence was EUR 81 120. Four entities were convicted of breach of trust in economic business (CA Art. 246) and received an average fine of EUR 3 900. Five other entities were fined an average of EUR 6 240 for tax or customs duties evasion (CA Art. 256).

Figure 6.2. Average fines against legal persons (2015-2019)

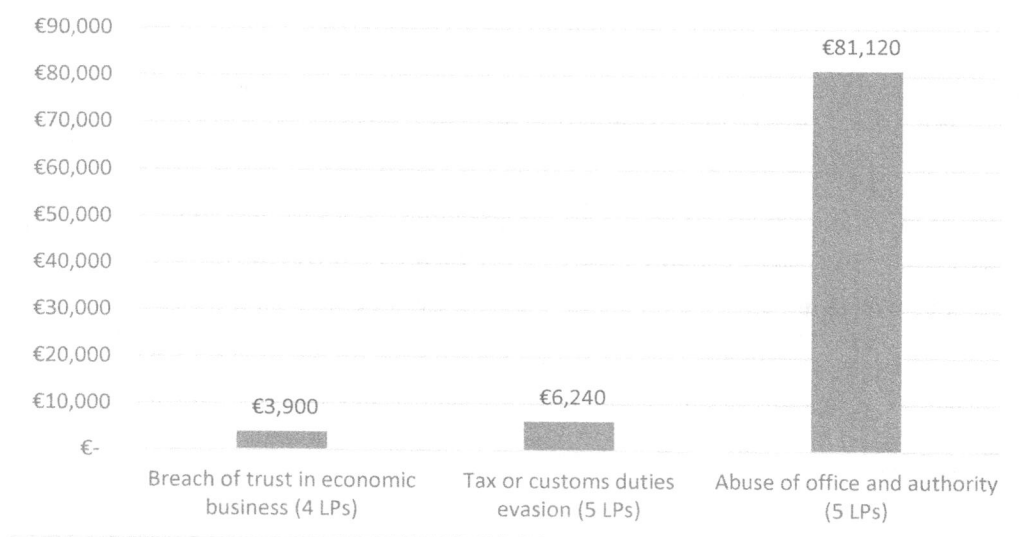

Source: USKOK.

6.3. Seizure and confiscation

Convention Art. 3 requires each Party to provide that the bribe and the proceeds of foreign bribery, or property the value of which corresponds to that of such proceeds, are subject to seizure and confiscation or that monetary sanctions of comparable effect are applicable. Commentary 21 elaborates that the "proceeds" of bribery are the profits or other benefits derived by the briber from the transaction or other improper advantage obtained or retained through bribery. Commentary 22 states that "confiscation" includes forfeiture where applicable, and means the permanent deprivation of property by order of a court or other competent authority.

6.3.1. Seizure

The Criminal Procedure Act (CPA) governs the seizure of the bribe and the proceeds of bribery.[9] Items subject to confiscation must be seized (CPA Art. 556(1)). The prosecutor may seek "insurance by any temporary measure" to preserve such items (CPA Art. 557a). Measures include freezing of bank accounts; seizure of cash and securities; and prohibition of the transfer of real property or real property rights. Measures are judicially reviewed every three months (CPA Art. 557e(3)). With some exceptions, they may last for a maximum of two years, extendable by the State Attorney for 60 days (CPA Art. 557e(2)).

6.3.2. Confiscation

CA Art. 5 states that "no one may retain the proceeds of an illegal act". CA Art. 77 provides for the confiscation of the proceeds of crime against natural persons in Croatia. A "property gain" must be confiscated upon a court decision that an unlawful act has been committed. Confiscation also applies to persons who do not acquire the property gain in good faith. Where the property gain cannot be confiscated, the court must order the perpetrator to pay an equivalent monetary amount. A court may decide not to order confiscation if the property gain is insignificant.

Confiscation of the bribe against natural persons is covered by CA Art. 79. The court may seize objects and means that are intended or used for the commission of an offence. Confiscation may be imposed even when the perpetrator of the unlawful act is not convicted.

These provisions are also applicable against legal persons. CLL Art. 19 states that the provisions of the Criminal Act and special laws on the confiscation of property gain and of objects apply to legal persons.

Croatia provided statistics on the application of confiscation covering cases of all crimes within USKOK's competence and not only active bribery. In 2015-2019, the Office for the Suppression of Corruption and Organised Crime (USKOK) obtained on average annually HRK 34.4 million (EUR 4.56 million) in confiscation against 112.5 persons. The amount confiscated was unusually high in 2018. If the data from this year is omitted, the average annual amount of confiscation falls to HRK 20.2 million (EUR 2.7 million).

Table 1. Confiscation of proceeds of offences within USKOK's competence (2015-19)

Year	Number of persons from whom proceeds were confiscated	Value (HRK)	Value (EUR)
2015	120	7 903 603.00	1 027 468.39
2016	95	16 876 824.25	2 193 987.15
2017	114	37 315 266.07	4 850 984.59
2018	138	89 422 969.01	11 624 985.97
2019	121	20 663 018.59	2 686 192.42
Total	588	172 181 680.92	22 383 618.52

Source: USKOK.

6.4. Penalties and mutual legal assistance / penalties and extradition

Sanctions for foreign bribery in Croatia are sufficient to enable effective mutual legal assistance (MLA) and extradition. The Mutual Legal Assistance in Criminal Matters Act does not limit the seeking of MLA and extradition to offences with a particular level of penalties. As mentioned at para. 0, foreign bribery to breach official duties is punishable by imprisonment of one to eight years, and by six months to five years for bribery to perform one's duty. This should be sufficient for most if not all bilateral and multilateral extradition and mutual legal assistance treaties, as well as the legislation for non-treaty-based international co-operation in foreign countries.

6.5. Additional civil and administrative sanctions

Convention Art. 3(4) requires countries to consider imposing additional civil or administrative sanctions for foreign bribery. Commentary 24 states that such sanctions may include the exclusion from entitlement to public benefits or aid; temporary or permanent disqualification from participation in public procurement or from the practice of other commercial activities; placing under judicial supervision; and a judicial winding-up order. The 2009 Recommendation XI.i further asks countries to suspend enterprises that have committed foreign bribery from competition for public contracts or other public advantages. If procurement sanctions are applied to enterprises for domestic bribery, then they should be applied equally to cases of foreign bribery.

Croatia provides for mandatory debarment from procurement contracts against individuals and companies convicted of foreign bribery. Under the Public Procurement Act 2016[10] Art. 251(1)(1)(b), an economic entity established in Croatia is excluded from a public procurement procedure if it or its representative has been convicted of bribery under CA Art. 294. Debarment is for five years unless a final judgment specifies otherwise (Art. 255(6)). However, an economic operator convicted of bribery may nevertheless avoid debarment if it proves its "reliability" (Art. 255(1)-(2)). Reliability is assessed in light of the entity's compensation of damages caused by the criminal offence, active cooperation with the investigators, and adoption of appropriate organisational measures to prevent further offences.

CLL Art. 17 allows for additional administrative sanctions against legal persons. A legal person may be banned from acquiring permits, authorisations, concessions or subsidies issued by state bodies or units of local and regional self-government. A ban is between one to three years. However, a ban may be imposed only if the acquisition of the permit, etc. could be "an incentive to [commit a] criminal offence". Croatian authorities explain that a ban would therefore only be imposed if there is a danger that the legal person commits further offences.

A legal person may also be judicially wound up as a sanction for foreign bribery. Under CLL Art. 12, a legal person may be terminated if it is established for the purpose of committing offences or its predominant activity is to commit offences. A fine may be imposed in addition to termination.

6.6. Conclusions on the sanctions for foreign bribery in Croatia

Croatia provides a range of sanctions against natural and legal persons for foreign bribery, including imprisonment (for natural persons), fines, confiscation and debarment. To further improve this regime, Croatia could consider the following:

a   Increase the maximum fines available against natural and legal persons for foreign bribery;

b   Take steps to ensure that the sanctions imposed against natural and legal persons in practice are effective, proportionate and dissuasive; and

c   Maintain detailed statistics on the sanctions, including on the amount of fines, as well as on confiscation and debarment that have been imposed in domestic and foreign bribery cases.

References

OECD (2015), *Greece Phase 3bis Report*, https://www.oecd.org/daf/anti-bribery/Greece-Phase-3bis-Report-EN.pdf#page=22&zoom=100,76,316. [4]

OECD (2014), *Argentina Phase 3 Report*, https://www.oecd.org/daf/anti-bribery/Argentina-Phase-3-Report-ENG.pdf#page=19&zoom=100,82,200. [1]

OECD (2014), *Chile Phase 3 Report*, https://www.oecd.org/daf/anti-bribery/ChilePhase3ReportEN.pdf#page=23&zoom=100,76,150. [6]

OECD (2013), *Belgium Phase 3 Report*, https://www.oecd.org/daf/anti-bribery/BelgiumPhase3ReportEN.pdf#page=21&zoom=100,82,100. [2]

OECD (2013), *Poland Phase 3 Report*, https://www.oecd.org/daf/anti-bribery/Polandphase3reportEN.pdf. [10]

OECD (2012), *France Phase 3 Report*, https://www.oecd.org/daf/anti-bribery/Francephase3reportEN.pdf#page=26&zoom=100,82,200. [3]

OECD (2012), *Netherlands Phase 3 Report*, https://www.oecd.org/daf/anti-bribery/NetherlandsphaseЗreportEN.pdf#page=20&zoom=100,82,400. [9]

OECD (2012), *Sweden Phase 3 Report*, https://www.oecd.org/daf/anti-bribery/SwedenphaseЗreportEN.pdf#page=22&zoom=100,76,333. [11]

OECD (2011), *Bulgaria Phase 3 Report*, https://www.oecd.org/daf/anti-bribery/anti-briberyconvention/BulgariaphaseЗreportEN.pdf. [5]

OECD (2011), *Germany Phase 3 Report*, https://www.oecd.org/daf/anti-bribery/anti-briberyconvention/GermanyphaseЗreportEN.pdf#page=36&zoom=100,82,225. [7]

OECD (2011), *Italy Phase 3 Report*, https://www.oecd.org/daf/anti-bribery/anti-briberyconvention/ItalyphaseЗreportEN.pdf#page=20&zoom=100,82,275. [8]

Notes

[1] For example, see (OECD, 2014[1]), para. 55 and Recommendation 4(a); (OECD, 2013[2]), paras. 39-40 and Recommendation 3(b); (OECD, 2012[3]), para. 58 and Recommendation 3(a); (OECD, 2015[4]), para. 66 and Recommendation 5(a).

[2] Corruption cases can be resolved without trial. Under the CPA, the defendant and the Prosecutor can conclude an agreement on guilt and punishment, which is then validated by the court (CPA Arts. 360-361).

[3] The cases mentioned are not included in the statistics provided by USKOK because the investigations were initiated before 2014.

[4] See also Tportal (5 April 2019), last accessed on 1 April 2021.

[5] Financial Times (30 December 2019), last accessed on 1 April 2021; N1 Info (25 October 2021), last accessed on 7 February 2022; MOLGroup, press release (25 October 2021), last accessed on 7 February 2022.

[6] For example, see (OECD, 2011[5]), paras. 40-41 and Recommendation 3(a); (OECD, 2013[10]), paras. 61-64 and Recommendation 3(a).

[7] For example, see (OECD, 2011[5]), para. 45 and Recommendation 3(c); (OECD, 2014[6]), para. 72 and Recommendation 3(d); (OECD, 2012[3]), para. 62 and Recommendation 3(b); (OECD, 2011[7]), paras. 100-102 and Recommendation 3(d); (OECD, 2015[4]), paras. 70-72 and Recommendation 5(c); (OECD, 2011[8]), paras. 61-62 and Recommendation 3(b); (OECD, 2012[9]), paras. 46-49 and

Recommendation 4(a); (OECD, 2013[10]), para. 65 and Recommendation 3(c); (OECD, 2012[11]), para. 56 and Recommendation 2.

[8] The offence of abuse of office and authority (CA Art. 291), when the offender has obtained substantial property benefit or caused significant damage, carries higher penalties than those available for active bribery.

[9] Criminal Procedure Act (*Zakon o kaznenom postupku*), Official Gazette No. 152/08, 76/09, 80/11, 121/11, 91/12, 143/12, 56/13, 145/13, 152/14, 70/17, 126/19, 126/19.

[10] Public Procurement Act (*Zakon o javnoj nabavi*), Official Gazette no. 120/2016.

7 Enforcement capacity

This chapter analyses Croatia's track record of investigating and prosecuting domestic and foreign corruption cases, including cases against legal persons. It also addresses other matters that may be relevant to Croatia's capacity to enforce its foreign bribery laws.

The fourth accession criterion related to the legal and enforcement framework to fight foreign bribery concerns the capacity to enforce foreign bribery laws. Under this criterion, the OECD Working Group on Bribery assesses: (i) whether a country has a track record of investigating and prosecuting domestic and foreign corruption cases; and (ii) any other matter relevant to a country's capacity to enforce its foreign bribery laws which raises significant concerns.

7.1. OECD standards on foreign bribery enforcement

Art. 5 of the Convention sets the standard on foreign bribery enforcement:

> *Enforcement*
>
> *Investigation and prosecution of the bribery of a foreign public official shall be subject to the applicable rules and principles of each Party. They shall not be influenced by considerations of national economic interest, the potential effect upon relations with another State or the identity of the natural or legal persons involved.*

Additional guidance is found in Commentary 27 and the 2009 Anti-Bribery Recommendation Annex I.D. These documents require competent authorities to seriously investigate complaints of foreign bribery, and that adequate resources are provided to permit effective prosecution of such crimes.

7.2. Rules and principles on investigations and prosecutions

In Croatia, the investigation and prosecution of corruption offences, including domestic and foreign bribery, fall under the exclusive jurisdiction of the Office for the Suppression of Corruption and Organised Crime (USKOK). The State Attorney is the public prosecutor of criminal offences in Croatia. USKOK is a specialised State Attorney's office that was established in 2001. Its jurisdiction is set out in Art. 21 of the Act on the Office for the Suppression of Corruption and Organised Crime (USKOK Act).[1] This includes active and passive foreign and domestic bribery, as well as other corruption offences.[2] The National Police Office for the Suppression of Corruption and Organised Crime (PNUSKOK) supports USKOK's investigations. USKOK cases are heard in four County Courts.[3]

The Criminal Procedure Act (CPA) and the Corporate Liability Law (CLL) set out the rules for investigating and prosecuting foreign bribery against natural and legal persons. The USKOK Act provides additional rules for USKOK's cases. The main stages of a corruption case are generally: preliminary proceedings, formal investigation, trial before the County Court, and appeals to the High Criminal Court and Supreme Court.[4]

The principle of "mandatory prosecution" applies with some qualifications. Unless otherwise prescribed by law, the State Attorney must initiate criminal proceedings if there is a reasonable suspicion that a criminal offence prosecutable *ex officio* has been committed (CPA Art. 2(3)). However, prosecutors can dismiss a report of a crime with a reasoned decision if there are insufficient grounds to conduct an investigation (CPA Art. 206). In subsequent stages, they may also file the investigation or drop the charges for lack of grounds (CPA Arts. 224, 380, 452). Prosecutors can reject a criminal report or drop charges against a legal person that has no or insignificant assets, or is subject to bankruptcy proceedings (CLL Art. 24).

7.3. Track record of investigating and prosecuting domestic and foreign corruption cases

Under the criteria for acceding to the Convention, the OECD Working Group on Bribery assesses a country's enforcement track record over a previous five-year period. Particular emphasis is given to foreign bribery cases, politically sensitive cases, cases impacting national economic interests, enforcement actions for active (as opposed to passive) corruption, and enforcement actions against legal persons.

7.3.1. Record of foreign bribery enforcement

As mentioned in Chapter 3, Croatian companies are active in countries with substantial levels of corruption, and are thus at risk of committing foreign bribery. Nevertheless, USKOK has never had a foreign bribery investigation or prosecution.

There has been at least one foreign bribery allegation implicating the representative of a Croatian company since 2015. According to media reports, a Monaco-based energy consulting firm allegedly paid EUR 2.5 million to the general manager of a Croatian state-owned oil company in Syria. The funds would then be used to bribe high-officials in Syria to win two gas plant contracts in the country for a client of the consulting firm. The general manager of the Croatian company has Syrian nationality and was also Croatia's honorary consul in Damascus.[5]

Croatian authorities became aware of these allegations in 2017 but did not conduct any investigations. The prosecutors at the fact-finding mission explain that the allegation did not relate to the activities of the Croatian state-owned company. Croatian authorities did not inquire whether the company benefited from the transaction. Nor did they consider whether they had jurisdiction over the company general manager's alleged acts. For example, Croatian authorities did not inquire whether the manager also had Croatian nationality that would subject him to extraterritorial jurisdiction under Croatian law. After reviewing a draft of this report, the Croatian Ministry of Justice and Public Administration states that, according to the information available on the case, there was no legal basis for further action by the Croatian authorities.

A second foreign bribery allegation surfaced in November 2021. According to media reports,[6] a Croatian company agreed in 2004 to purchase used weapons from the Bosnian government. Sometime in 2009-2011, Bosnia and Herzegovina's then-defence minister allegedly altered the terms of the contract in favour of the Croatian company without authorisation. In November 2021, Bosnian authorities charged the minister with corruption and abuse of office over the transaction. USKOK states that its only information on the case is from media reports, which do not refer to "bribery". Based on this information, USKOK believes that "the matter falls within the jurisdiction of the judicial authorities of Bosnia and Herzegovina, and that the judicial authorities of the Republic of Croatia have no jurisdiction in this matter". USKOK further states that it "has received no request issued by any foreign judicial authority to provide assistance or information regarding" this case. It is unclear why USKOK has not considered exercising Croatia's jurisdiction over the foreign bribery offence in CA Art. 294 committed by Croatian nationals and companies. No efforts have been made, for example, to determine whether part of the alleged foreign bribery took place in Croatia.

7.3.2. Record of enforcement of domestic bribery and other cases

USKOK has a stronger track record in domestic corruption enforcement. Croatian authorities provided data on USKOK cases in 2015-2019 against natural persons for three categories of offences: active and passive bribery in business dealings (CA Arts. 252 and 253), active and passive bribery (CA Arts. 293 and 294), and trading in influence (CA Arts. 295 and 296). For these three categories of corruption offences:

- USKOK investigated 285 individuals (193 for active and 92 for passive corruption) and indicted 306 individuals (202 for active and 104 for passive corruption).
- The courts decided 323 cases: 304 convictions (168 for active and 136 for passive corruption) and 19 acquittals (10 for active and 9 for passive corruption).
- 219 of the convictions (72%) resulted from a non-trial resolution (138 for active and 81 for passive corruption).

In recent years, USKOK has also had several high-level corruption cases, including five against a former Prime Minister. An evaluation by another international organisation found that USKOK has a solid track record of investigating and prosecuting high-level corruption, "with several indictments filed against persons who formerly held top executive functions".[7]

7.3.3. Record of corporate enforcement

In 2015-2019, USKOK did not initiate or conclude any cases against legal persons for any bribery or trading in influence offences (CA Arts. 253, 294 and 296). However, it took enforcement action for other offences including fraud (CA Art. 236), breach of trust in economic business (CA Art. 246), tax or customs duties evasion (CA Art. 256), and abuse of office and authority (CA Art. 291):

- USKOK investigated 106 legal persons and indicted 72 legal persons.
- The courts decided 19 cases and entered 15 convictions.
- of the convictions (or 60%) resulted from non-trial resolutions.

Information on additional high-level corruption cases paints a similar picture. In the *Planinska* case, a former parliamentarian and his two companies paid the then-Prime Minister to secure a property sale. The companies were convicted of incitement to commit abuse of office and authority (CA Arts. 37 and 291(2)).[8] In the *HEP/Dioki* and *INA/MOL* cases, legal persons were involved but not indicted.

The complete absence of corporate enforcement of bribery offences is striking for two reasons. First, over the same period, USKOK investigated and indicted hundreds of natural persons for these crimes. It is surprising that none of these cases resulted in investigations or prosecutions of legal persons. Second, USKOK investigated and indicted many legal persons for non-bribery offences during this time, which demonstrates a willingness and ability for corporate enforcement. Why this does not extend to bribery offences is unclear.

Participants at the fact-finding mission offered a range of explanations for the lack of corporate enforcement of bribery offences. Prosecutors cite the difficulty of proving an "illegal property gain" under the CLL (see Section 5.5). This was the reason why legal persons were not prosecuted in the *INA/MOL* case. Parliamentarians and a private sector representative note that it seems easier for prosecutors to charge individuals than companies. Parliamentarians add that corporate enforcement is pointless because companies usually have insufficient assets or are bankrupt. However, that USKOK has actively enforced non-bribery offences against companies would seem to refute all of these explanations.

The OECD Working Group on Bribery has observed that the prosecution of legal persons is a horizontal issue that affects several Parties to the Convention. It has recommended that Parties draw the attention of prosecutors to the importance of applying effectively the liability of legal persons in foreign bribery cases.[9]

7.4. Other matters relating to enforcement capacity

Under the fourth accession criterion, the OECD Working Group on Bribery also considers any other matter relevant to a country's capacity to enforce its foreign bribery laws that raises significant concerns. This report considers two issues: executive interference in investigations and prosecutions, and delay in proceedings.

7.4.1. Executive interference in investigations and prosecutions

Croatia's legal system has several formal guarantees of judicial and prosecutorial independence. The Constitution and statute provide for autonomy and independence of the Judiciary and State Attorney's

Council. Deputy State Attorneys are independent in their work. Influence and coercion of State Attorneys and Deputy State Attorneys are prohibited.[10]

Despite these provisions, the judiciary is perceived to lack independence. According to a 2020 European Commission report, the level of perceived judicial independence in Croatia among companies is the second lowest in the EU. Among the general public, it is the lowest, with only 24% of respondents perceiving judicial independence to be fairly or very good. This figure dropped to 17% in the following year. The main reason cited by the general public for their opinion is the perception of interference or pressure from the government and politicians.[11]

Only some of the fact-finding mission participants share these views. Civil society representatives and one parliamentarian question the State Attorney's independence, especially in high-level corruption cases. They also criticise the process for appointing the State Attorney General and President of the Supreme Court. Other participants are critical of a Constitutional Court decision in a corruption case against a former Prime Minister. But none of the participants describes specific instances of political interference or a lack of independence in corruption cases.

Other fact-finding mission participants, particularly those in the judiciary and law enforcement, are more positive about judicial independence. Judges acknowledge the public's perception of their lack of independence. But they insist that they have not personally been subject to political interference or heard of colleagues with such experiences. They also argue that trials and appeals are heard by three-judge panels and thus difficult to influence. Likewise, prosecutors and investigators state that they have not been subject to undue interference, even in complex corruption investigations. They believe that a vertical hierarchy in their institutions enhances independence. Prosecutors also refer to USKOK's track record of corruption cases, including convictions of high-level officials such as a former Prime Minister. Representatives of academia, the legal profession, and the private sector also think that these cases attest to USKOK's independence.

7.4.2. Delay in criminal proceedings

The 2020 and 2021 European Commission reports mentioned above also criticise Croatia for protracted criminal proceedings. Although investigations in 2020 took longer owing to case complexity and the COVID-19 pandemic, overall investigations appear relatively speedy. In 2019, "USKOK received and resolved a larger number of cases, and registered a declining number of unresolved cases". About 90% of its investigations took up to 6 months to complete, down from 12 months in 2016. However, "considerable backlogs and lengthy proceedings" in the criminal justice system are a challenge. USKOK has encountered "issues with the inefficiency of the justice system, where lengthy court proceedings and appeals often impede closure of cases." From 2019 to 2020, backlogs and average length of proceedings increased in first instance cases at Municipal courts from 691 to 705 days. The figure for County courts is even higher (804 in 2020).[12]

Participants at the fact-finding mission agree with these findings, especially in high-level corruption cases. Journalists, representatives of civil society, and a parliamentarian state that final sentences in high-level corruption cases take a long time. This fuels a public perception that enforcement is selective and favours low-level corruption. Information provided by Croatian authorities points to the same conclusion. Of the five corruption cases brought against a former Prime Minister, one was concluded after seven years. The others were opened in 2010-2011. Of these, three were concluded with Supreme Court decisions in October-November 2021 (two convictions and one acquittal). The defendants may still challenge the decisions before the Constitutional Court, however. One other case is still ongoing at the time of this report.

Fact-finding mission participants proffer two explanations for the delay. First, prosecutors, judges, academics and lawyers blame the complexity of these corruption cases, which usually have multiple defendants and frequent amendments to the indictments. Additional complication results from complex facts, the amount of evidence including documentation, numerous witnesses and expert opinions, according to the Ministry of Justice and Public Administration. Recent amendments to criminal procedure have helped but certain issues remain. One law professor cited as an example certain rules on appeal that often lead to retrials. Second, judges state they have very limited resources and significant caseloads. One judge believes creating a court specialising in USKOK cases would improve efficiency. But such a measure would increase susceptibility to political interference, according to a parliamentarian.

Protracted corruption cases are an issue faced by Parties to the Convention. The OECD Working Group on Bribery has therefore recommended that these countries take steps to effectively reduce delay in these cases.[13]

7.5. Conclusion on enforcement in Croatia

Croatia has a track record of enforcing domestic bribery offences against natural persons. Available data indicate hundreds of investigations, indictments and convictions for these crimes in 2015-2019. However, there was no such similar enforcement against natural persons for foreign bribery over the same period. Also absent was enforcement against legal persons for foreign and domestic bribery. To strengthen its enforcement record, Croatia could consider the following:

a Enhance enforcement of the domestic and foreign bribery offences against natural and legal persons whenever appropriate; and

b Take steps to reduce delay in criminal proceedings in corruption cases.

References

OECD (2017), *Argentina Phase 3bis Report*, http://www.oecd.org/corruption/anti-bribery/Argentina-Phase-3bis-Report-ENG.pdf#page=15&zoom=100,76,633. [7]

OECD (2015), *Israel Phase 3 Report*, https://www.oecd.org/daf/anti-bribery/Israel-Phase-3-Report-ENG.pdf. [9]

OECD (2014), *Argentina Phase 3 Report*, https://www.oecd.org/daf/anti-bribery/Argentina-Phase-3-Report-ENG.pdf#page=14&zoom=100,82,200. [6]

OECD (2014), *Chile Phase 3 Report*, https://www.oecd.org/daf/anti-bribery/ChilePhase3ReportEN.pdf#page=23&zoom=100,76,150. [4]

OECD (2014), *Turkey Phase 3 Report*, https://www.oecd.org/daf/anti-bribery/TurkeyPhase3ReportEN.pdf. [3]

OECD (2013), *Denmark Phase 3 Report*, https://www.oecd.org/daf/anti-bribery/Denmarkphase3reportEN.pdf. [2]

OECD (2013), *Portugal Phase 3 Report*, https://www.oecd.org/daf/anti-bribery/Portugalphase3reportEN.pdf. [5]

OECD (2012), *Greece Phase 2 Report*, https://www.oecd.org/daf/anti-bribery/anti-briberyconvention/35140946.pdf. [8]

OECD (2012), *Netherlands Phase 3 Report*, https://www.oecd.org/daf/anti-bribery/Netherlandsphase3reportEN.pdf#page=20&zoom=100,82,400.

[1]

Notes

[1] Act on the Office for the Suppression of Corruption and Organised Crime (*Zakon o Uredu za suzbijanje korupcije i organiziranog kriminaliteta*), (USKOK Act), Official Gazette no. 76/09, 116/10, 145/10, 57/11, 136/12, 148/13, 70/17.

[2] These include taking and giving bribes in bankruptcy proceedings (CA Art. 251), taking bribes in business dealings (CA Art. 252), giving bribes in business dealings (CA Art. 253), abuse of office and official authority (CA Art. 291) if committed by an official person under CA Art. 87(3), illegal intercession (CA Art. 292), taking bribes (CA Art. 293), giving bribes (Art. 294), trading in influence (CA Art. 295), giving bribes for trading in influence (CA Art. 296), and bribing elected representatives (CA Art. 339) (USKOK Act Art. 21(2)(1)).

[3] USKOK Act, Art. 31.

[4] Criminal Procedure Act, Articles 19.c(1)(b), 19.e(1)(1), and 19.f(1), 205, 216-217, 341-343, 367; USKOK Act Arts. 24 and 29(2). The "High Criminal Court" was instituted with an amendment to the CPA in 2008, and should hear appeals against first-instance County Court rulings. Its establishment was suspended pending a constitutional challenge, but resumed as of 1 January 2021 as decided by the Constitutional Court. See Total Croatia News (3 November 2020), "Const. Court Decides High Criminal Court to Start Working on 1 Jan 2021".

[5] The Age and Huffpost, The Bribe Factory: World's Biggest Bribe Scandal (last accessed on 26 March 2021).

[6] Reuters (26 November 2021), "Bosnian security minister indicted over corruption allegations"; Balkan Insight (29 November 2021), "Former Bosnian Defence Minister Indicted for Abuse of Office" (both last accessed 14 February 2022).

[7] GRECO (2019), Evaluation Report of Croatia, Fifth Round, GrecoEval5Rep(2019)1, paras. 13 and 100.

[8] Tportal (5 April 2019), last accessed on 1 April 2021.

[9] For example, see (OECD, 2012[1]), paras. 34-35 and Recommendations 2(b) and 3(b); (OECD, 2013[2]), paras. 75-76 and Recommendation 2(a); (OECD, 2014[3]), paras. 49-51 and Recommendation 1(d); (OECD, 2014[4]), paras. 92-103 and Recommendation 4(c)(i); (OECD, 2015[9]), Recommendation 3(b)(iii); (OECD, 2013[5]), paras. 93-95 and Recommendation 5(c)(iv).

[10] Constitution Arts. 115 and 121a; State Attorney's Office Act Arts. 5-6; CA Art. 312.

[11] European Commission (30 September 2020), 2020 Rule of Law Report - Country Chapter on the rule of law situation in Croatia, SWD(2020) 310 final, pp. 2-3; and European Commission (20 July 2021), 2021 Rule of Law Report - Country Chapter on the rule of law situation in Croatia, SWD(2021) 713 final, pp. 2-3.

[12] European Commission (30 September 2020), 2020 Rule of Law Report - Country Chapter on the rule of law situation in Croatia, SWD(2020) 310 final, pp. 8 and 13; and European Commission (20 July 2021), 2021 Rule of Law Report - Country Chapter on the rule of law situation in Croatia, SWD(2021) 713 final, pp. 8-9 and 11.

[13] For example, see (OECD, 2014[6]), paras. 86-99 and Recommendation 5(c); (OECD, 2017[7]), paras. 81-87 and Recommendation 5(e); (OECD, 2012[8]), para. 154-156 and 215(c).

8 International co-operation

This chapter reviews Croatia's framework for seeking and providing mutual legal assistance and extradition to determine whether it is in line with the standards set out in the OECD Anti-Bribery Convention.

International co-operation is the fifth accession criterion on the legal and legislative framework for fighting foreign bribery. The OECD Working Group on Bribery assesses an accession candidate's framework for seeking and providing mutual legal assistance (MLA) and extradition against Arts. 9 and 10 of the Convention. The Working Group also considers any other information that comes to its attention and which is relevant to the candidate's capacity to seek and provide MLA and extradition.

8.1. Mutual legal assistance

Convention Art. 9(1) requires countries to provide prompt and effective legal assistance for the purpose of criminal investigations and proceedings of offences within the scope of the Convention. Assistance should also be provided for non-criminal proceedings within the scope of the Convention brought against a legal person.

8.1.1. Laws, treaties and arrangements for mutual legal assistance

Croatia is party to the following multilateral treaties that provide for MLA in foreign bribery cases: the European Convention on Mutual Assistance in Criminal Matters; United Nations Convention against Corruption; and United Nations Convention against Transnational Organized Crime. Croatia indicates that it is also party to bilateral MLA treaties with Austria, Bosnia and Herzegovina, Kosovo, Montenegro, North Macedonia, Serbia, and Slovenia. A bilateral MLA treaty with Turkey is signed but not in force. Croatia provides MLA in respect of "international and supranational organisations whose member the Republic of Croatia may become, if so stipulated in an international treaty" (Art. 1(5) of the Mutual Legal Assistance in Criminal Matters Act, MLACMA). Croatian authorities state that, if Croatia accedes to the OECD Anti-Bribery Convention, it would accept Convention Art. 9 as a basis for seeking and providing MLA in foreign bribery cases.

MLA with EU member countries is governed by separate legislation, the Judicial Co-operation in Criminal Matters Act with the Member States of the European Union. Croatia implemented the European Investigation Order in 2017 (European Judicial Network, 2017[1]).

Non-treaty-based MLA is governed by the MLACMA. Art. 4 states that MLA "is afforded in the widest sense, in compliance with the principles of domestic legal order, principles of the European Convention for the Protection of Human Rights and Fundamental Freedoms and the International Covenant on Civil and Political Rights." Art. 3(1)(1) describes the types of assistance available, namely "procuring and transmitting articles to be produced in evidence, service of writs and records of judicial verdicts, appearance before the court of witnesses for testimony and other acts necessary to carry out the court proceedings".

MLACMA Art. 6 sets out the authorities and channels for communicating MLA requests. The Ministry of Justice and Public Administration (MOJ) is the central authority for sending and receiving requests. Urgent requests may be communicated through Interpol. The MOJ sends and receives requests through the diplomatic channel unless a treaty provides otherwise. Croatian judicial authorities may exceptionally send MLA requests directly to foreign authorities where explicitly permitted by treaty or the MLACMA. In such cases, the judicial authority provides a copy of the request to the MOJ.

8.1.2. Dual criminality for mutual legal assistance

Convention Art. 9(2) states that, where a country makes MLA conditional upon the existence of dual criminality, the condition is deemed to have been met if the offence for which the assistance is sought is within the scope of the Convention.

Croatian authorities state that dual criminality is required for MLA, despite the absence of an express provision stipulating this requirement in the MLACMA. Croatia executes an MLA request "provided that both countries criminalise the conduct underlying the offence, regardless of whether both countries place the offence within the same category of offence or denominate the offence by the same terminology".

Croatia cannot provide MLA for non-criminal proceedings for foreign bribery brought by foreign authorities against a legal person. Under the MLACMA, MLA is provided "in respect of criminal acts" (Art. 1(2)). It is also available "in misdemeanour proceedings brought by the administrative authorities, in respect of acts which are punishable under the Croatian law by pecuniary fine, by virtue of being infringements of the rule of law and where in such proceedings the decision of the administrative authority may give rise to proceedings before a court having subject matter jurisdiction in criminal matters" (Art. 1(3)). This provision likely would not apply to foreign administrative proceedings against legal persons for foreign bribery.

The issue of providing MLA for non-criminal proceedings within the scope of the Anti-Bribery Convention brought against a legal person has arisen in Parties to the Convention. The OECD Working Group on Bribery has thus recommended that countries ensure that a broad range of MLA, including coercive measures, can be provided in foreign bribery-related civil or administrative proceedings against a legal person to a foreign state whose legal system does not allow criminal liability of legal persons.[1]

8.1.3. Other grounds of refusal

Convention Art. 9(3) states that a country shall not decline to render mutual legal assistance for criminal matters within the scope of the Convention on the ground of bank secrecy. No other grounds of denial are mentioned in the Convention.

MLACMA Arts. 12-13 set out the grounds for refusal. MLA may be denied for a political offence, a fiscal offence or an insignificant criminal offence. It may also be refused if a request would prejudice the sovereignty, security, legal order or other essential interests of Croatia. Requests must be refused if the absolute statute of limitations has expired, or if criminal proceedings are pending in Croatia against the prosecuted person for the same criminal offence.

Ne bis in idem is also a mandatory ground for denying MLA, although the definition of this concept may be overbroad. Under MLACMA Art. 13(1), a request must be refused if the accused has been acquitted in Croatia for the same offence based on the substantive-legal grounds; if he/she was acquitted of the punishment; or if a sanction was executed or may not be executed pursuant to the law of the country in which the verdict has been passed. However, the provision also requires MLA to be denied "if a procedure against [the accused] has been discontinued". Croatian authorities state that this refers to the suspension of criminal proceedings in Art. 380 of the Criminal Procedure Act. This provision allows proceedings to be suspended on grounds other than the merits, such as when the prosecutor drops the charge, or if there are "other circumstances that preclude criminal prosecution".

8.2. Extradition

Convention Art. 10(1) provides that foreign bribery shall be deemed to be included as an extraditable offence under the laws of the Parties and the extradition treaties between them. Art. 10(2) states that, if a Party which makes extradition conditional on the existence of an extradition treaty receives a request for extradition from another Party with which it has no extradition treaty, it may consider this Convention to be the legal basis for extradition in respect of the offence of bribery of a foreign public official.

8.2.1. Laws and treaties for extradition

Croatia is party to the following multilateral treaties that provide for extradition in foreign bribery cases: the European Convention on Extradition and additional protocols; United Nations Convention against Corruption; and United Nations Convention against Transnational Organized Crime. Croatia implemented the European Arrest Warrant. Croatia indicates that it is party to bilateral extradition treaties with Bosnia and Herzegovina, Montenegro, and North Macedonia. A treaty signed with Serbia is not yet in force but "provisionally applied", according to Croatia. Croatian authorities state that, if Croatia accedes to the OECD Anti-Bribery Convention, it would accept Convention Art. 10(2) as legal basis for extradition in foreign bribery cases.

In the absence of a treaty, extradition may be granted on the basis of reciprocity (MLACMA Art. 34(5)). Extraditable offences are those that are punishable by imprisonment of at least one year or a more severe penalty (Art. 34(2)). The Ministry of Justice and Public Administration is the central authority for incoming and outgoing extradition requests (Arts. 6(2) and 40). Incoming requests are transmitted to the competent court where the person sought is found (Art. 45). The court conducts a hearing to determine whether the statutory preconditions for extradition are met. The decision may be appealed to the Supreme Court (Arts. 55-56). If the courts allow extradition, the Minister of Justice decides whether to surrender the person sought (Art. 57). This procedure can be bypassed with the consent of the person sought (Art. 54).

8.2.2. Dual criminality for extradition and other grounds of refusal

Convention Art. 10(2) states that extradition for foreign bribery "is subject to the conditions set out in the domestic law and applicable treaties and arrangements of each Party. Where a Party makes extradition conditional upon the existence of dual criminality, that condition shall be deemed to be fulfilled if the offence for which extradition is sought is within the scope of Article 1 of this Convention."

Dual criminality is a precondition for extradition. MLACMA Art. 35(3) states that extradition is not allowed "if the offence for which extradition is claimed is not a criminal offence in both domestic law and the law of the state in which it was committed".

MLACMA Art. 35 sets out additional grounds for denying extradition. Extradition is refused if the underlying offence was committed on Croatian territory, or against Croatia or its national; the statute of limitations has expired; the person sought has been convicted or finally acquitted of the same offence by a court in the requesting state; Croatia has initiated criminal proceedings against the person sought for the same offence; if the identity of the person sought is not determined; or if there is insufficient evidence to establish a reasonable suspicion that the person sought committed the offence. Extradition may be refused if Croatia may take over the prosecution of an offence, and if this would be appropriate for the "social rehabilitation" of the person sought.

8.2.3. Extradition of nationals

Convention Art. 10(3) states that "each Party shall take any measures necessary to assure either that it can extradite its nationals or that it can prosecute its nationals for the offence of bribery of a foreign public official. A Party which declines a request to extradite a person for bribery of a foreign public official solely on the ground that the person is its national shall submit the case to its competent authorities for the purpose of prosecution."

Croatia does not extradite its nationals, apart from under a European Arrest Warrant or in accordance with an international treaty. MLACMA Arts. 32 and 35(1)(1) bar extradition of a Croatian national. No provision mandates Croatian authorities to prosecute a person whose extradition has been declined solely because of nationality. Under MLACMA Art. 62, a foreign judicial authority must request Croatia to take over criminal proceedings. The foreign judicial authority must also undertake not to prosecute the person after the final decision of their Croatian counterpart. A foreign request to prosecute is transmitted to the competent state attorney in Croatia (Art. 63(1)). A decision to refuse prosecution is relayed to the foreign judicial authority via the Croatian Ministry of Justice and Public Administration (Art. 63(3)). If prosecution proceeds, an offence committed abroad is considered to have taken place in Croatia, and foreign law applies if it is more lenient to the accused than Croatian law (Art. 64). Investigative actions taken by foreign authorities are considered to have been taken by Croatian ones (Art. 68).

The OECD Working Group on Bribery has recommended that Parties to the Convention ensure that cases that are declined for extradition solely on grounds of nationality are submitted to prosecution.[2] In particular, the Working Group has stated recently that prosecution in lieu of extradition only upon the demand of a foreign state does not meet the requirements of Convention Art. 10(3).[3]

8.3. Conclusions on international co-operation in foreign bribery cases

Croatia has treaty relations in extradition and MLA with many foreign countries, mainly resulting from multilateral conventions in these areas and from anti-corruption conventions that provide for international co-operation. In the absence of an applicable treaty, extradition and MLA is available on the basis of reciprocity. To strengthen this regime, Croatia could consider the following:

a   Provide a broad range of MLA, including coercive measures, in foreign bribery-related civil or administrative proceedings against a legal person to a foreign state whose legal system does not allow criminal liability of legal persons;

b   Ensure that MLA is not refused because of ne bis in idem in cases in which criminal proceedings in Croatia have been discontinued on grounds other than the merits; and

c   Ensure that cases that are declined for extradition solely on grounds of nationality are submitted to prosecution.

References

European Judicial Network (2017), *Notification of the transposition of Directive 2014/41/EU on European Investigation Order in criminal matters by Croatia*, https://www.ejn-crimjust.europa.eu/ejn/libdocumentproperties.aspx?Id=2065.   [1]

OECD (2020), *Costa Rica Phase 2 Report*, https://www.oecd.org/corruption/Costa Rica-Phase-2-Report-ENG.pdf#page=52&zoom=100,82,214.   [8]

OECD (2017), *Lithuania Phase 2 Report*, https://www.oecd.org/corruption/anti-bribery/Lithuania-Phase-2-Report-ENG.pdf#page=54&zoom=100,76,566.   [6]

OECD (2015), *Phase 2 Report on Implementing the OECD Anti-Bribery Convention in Latvia*, https://www.oecd.org/daf/anti-bribery/Latvia-Phase-2-Report-ENG.pdf#page=54&zoom=100,76,165.   [5]

OECD (2013), *New Zealand Phase 3 Report*, http://www.oecd.org/daf/anti-bribery/NewZealandPhase3ReportEN.pdf#page=39&zoom=100,80,350.   [4]

OECD (2012), *Australia Phase 3 Report*, https://www.oecd.org/daf/anti-bribery/Australiaphase3reportEN.pdf.   [2]

OECD (2012), *Spain Phase 3 Report*, https://www.oecd.org/daf/anti-bribery/Spainphase3reportEN.pdf#page=14&zoom=100,76,550.   [7]

OECD (2005), *Hungary Phase 2 Report*, https://www.oecd.org/daf/anti-bribery/anti-briberyconvention/34918600.pdf.

[3]

Notes

[1] For example, see (OECD, 2012[2]), paras. 124-126 and Recommendation 11; (OECD, 2005[3]), paras. 94 and 209(c).

[2] (OECD, 2013[4]), paras. 117-119 and Recommendation 8; (OECD, 2015[5]), paras. 187-188 and Recommendation 12(b); (OECD, 2017[6]), paras. 143-144 and Recommendation 9(b); (OECD, 2012[7]), para. 161 and Recommendation 7.

[3] (OECD, 2020[8]), paras. 192-194 and Recommendation 11(f).

9 Non-tax deductibility of bribes

This chapter assesses whether Croatia prohibits the tax deduction of bribes to foreign public officials for all tax purposes, and whether this prohibition is contained in an explicit provision.

9.1. OECD standards on the non-tax deductibility of bribes

The final criterion on the legal and institutional framework is the non-tax deductibility of bribes to foreign officials. The 2009 Anti-Bribery Recommendation VIII ask countries to "explicitly" prohibit such deductions:

> *Tax Deductibility*
>
> *VIII. URGES Member countries to:*
>
> *i) fully and promptly implement the Council Recommendation on Tax Measures for Further Combating Bribery of Foreign Public Officials in International Business Transactions (OECD, 2009[1]), which recommends in particular "that Member countries and other Parties to the OECD Anti-Bribery Convention explicitly disallow the tax deductibility of bribes to foreign public officials, for all tax purposes in an effective manner" [...].*

9.2. Tax deductibility of bribes in Croatia

Croatia's Profit Tax Act determines the tax payable on income or profits. Taxpayers include both natural and legal persons (Art. 2). The tax payable by a taxpayer is a function of its tax base (Art. 32). The tax base is the difference between a taxpayer's revenues and expenditures, subject to certain adjustments (Art. 5).[1]

Croatia prohibits the tax deduction of bribes, though not via an explicit provision. Under Profit Tax Act Art. 7(1)(9), the tax base is increased "by benefits and other forms of property benefits given to natural or legal persons for an event to take place or not take place, i.e. to perform a certain action, for example better or faster than usual, or for its non-performance". The tax effect of such benefits is therefore neutral. A taxpayer would record the benefit as an expenditure which reduces the tax base under Art. 5, only for the tax base to then increase by a corresponding amount under Art. 7(1)(9). Benefits under Art. 7(1)(9) cover bribes to foreign public officials, according to Croatian authorities. The combined effect of these provisions is therefore to prohibit the tax deduction of bribes. Croatian authorities are not aware of cases in which Art. 7(1)(9) was applied to a bribe, however.

The absence of an explicit prohibition on the tax deduction of bribes does not meet OECD standards. The OECD Working Group on Bribery has repeatedly recommended that countries enact an explicit, legally binding provision, regardless of whether bribes are deductible under pre-existing legislation.[2]

9.3. Conclusion

Croatia prohibits the tax deduction of bribes through a range of provisions in the Profit Tax Act. However, the 2009 Anti-Bribery Recommendation demands an explicit, legally binding provision on the non-deductibility of bribes. To strengthen its anti-foreign bribery framework, Croatia could consider enacting such a legislative provision.

References

OECD (2014), *Argentina Phase 3 Report*, https://www.oecd.org/daf/anti-bribery/Argentina-Phase-3-Report-ENG.pdf#page=14&zoom=100,82,200. [2]

OECD (2013), *Poland Phase 3 Report*, https://www.oecd.org/daf/anti-bribery/Polandphase3reportEN.pdf. [6]

OECD (2012), *Greece Phase 3 Report*, https://www.oecd.org/daf/anti-bribery/Greecephase3reportEN.pdf#page=34&zoom=100,82,560. [4]

OECD (2011), *Bulgaria Phase 3 Report*, https://www.oecd.org/daf/anti-bribery/anti-briberyconvention/Bulgariaphase3reportEN.pdf. [3]

OECD (2011), *Mexico Phase 3 Report*, https://www.oecd.org/daf/anti-bribery/Mexicophase3reportEN.pdf#page=28&zoom=100,82,640. [5]

OECD (2009), *Recommendation of the Council on Tax Measures for Further Combating Bribery of Foreign Public Officials in International Business Transactions*, https://www.oecd.org/daf/anti-bribery/44176910.pdf. [1]

OECD (2006), *Spain Phase 2 Report*, https://www.oecd.org/daf/anti-bribery/anti-briberyconvention/36392481.pdf#page=46&zoom=100,82,600. [12]

OECD (2005), *Belgium Phase 2 Report*, https://www.oecd.org/daf/anti-bribery/anti-briberyconvention/35461651.pdf#page=48&zoom=100,82,250. [7]

OECD (2005), *Japan Phase 2 Report*, https://www.oecd.org/daf/anti-bribery/anti-briberyconvention/34554382.pdf#page=24&zoom=100,82,350. [9]

OECD (2005), *Slovak Republic Phase 2*, https://www.oecd.org/daf/anti-bribery/anti-briberyconvention/35778308.pdf#page=30&zoom=100,76,433. [11]

OECD (2004), *France Phase 2 Report*, https://www.oecd.org/daf/anti-bribery/anti-briberyconvention/26242055.pdf#page=53&zoom=100,82,550. [8]

OECD (2004), *Korea Phase 2 Report*, https://www.oecd.org/daf/anti-bribery/anti-briberyconvention/33910834.pdf#page=15&zoom=100,82,400. [10]

Notes

[1] Profit Tax Act (*Zakon o Porezu na Dobit*), Official Gazette no. 177/04, 90/05, 57/06, 146/08, 80/10, 22/12, 148/13, 143/14, 50/16, 115/16, 106/18, 121/19, 32/20, 138/20.

[2] (OECD, 2014[2]), paras. 178-181 and Recommendation 11(a); (OECD, 2011[3]), paras. 86-90 and Recommendation 7(a); (OECD, 2012[4]), paras. 113-115 and Recommendation 12(a); (OECD, 2011[5]), paras. 89-91 and Recommendation 13(a); (OECD, 2013[6]), paras. 115-121 and Recommendation 7(a); (OECD, 2005[7]), paras. 166-173 and 179(p); (OECD, 2004[8]), paras. 142-148 and Recommendation 13; (OECD, 2005[9]), paras. 87-88 and Recommendation 13; (OECD, 2004[10]), paras. 40-41 and 145(a); (OECD, 2005[11]), paras. 58-60 and 238(a); (OECD, 2006[12]), paras. 157-164 and 182.

Annex A. Fact-finding mission participants

Public sector

Ministry of Justice and Public Administration

i.   Sector for Prevention of Corruption
ii. Directorate for Criminal Law
iii. Sector for International Judicial Cooperation

Ministry of Finance, Tax Administration

i.   Sector for Business Processes, Internal Audit and Internal Supervision
ii. Independent Sector for financial investigations
iii. Sector for Supervision

Judiciary and law enforcement

i.   Office for the Suppression of Corruption and Organised Crime (USKOK)
ii. National Police Office for the Suppression of Corruption and Organised Crime (PNUSKOK)
iii. County Court of Zagreb

Private sector, legal profession and academics

i.   Croatian Employers' Association
ii. University of Zagreb, Faculty of Law
iii. Croatian Bar Association

Civil society and media

i.   Croatian Journalists Association
ii. Electronic Media Agency
iii. Večernji list
iv. HRT Television
v.   Transparency International Croatia[1]

Parliamentarians

i.   Including members of the National Council for Monitoring the Implementation of the Anti-corruption Strategy

Notes

[1] Transparency International Hrvatska is an independent Croatian civil society association and not a national chapter of the NGO Transparency International.

Annex B. Excerpts of relevant legislation

Criminal Act

Chapter VII Meaning of terms in this law

Article 87

(3) An official is a state official or civil servant, an official or clerk in a unit of local and regional self-government, a holder of judicial office, a lay judge, a member of the State Judicial Council or the State Attorney's Council, an arbitrator, a notary public and a professional worker performing tasks of social work, education and training activities. An official is also a person who in the European Union, a foreign state, an international organisation of which the Republic of Croatia is a member, an international court or arbitration tribunal whose jurisdiction the Republic of Croatia accepts, performs duties entrusted to persons referred to in the previous sentence.

[…]

(6) A responsible person is a natural person who manages the affairs of a legal person or is explicitly or actually entrusted with the performance of activities in the field of activity of a legal person or state bodies or bodies of a local and regional self-government unit.

[…]

(22) The property gain from a criminal offence shall be deemed to be the direct property gain from a criminal offence, the assets into which the property gain has been changed or converted, as well as any other proceeds of direct proceeds of crime or property in which has changed or converted the direct property gain from the criminal offence, regardless of whether it is located in the territory of the Republic of Croatia or outside it.

(23) Property is considered to be property of any kind, regardless of whether it is tangible or intangible, movable or immovable, or legal documents or instruments proving the right to or interest in such property.

(24) A bribe is any undue reward, gift or other property or non-property benefit, regardless of value.

Article 294 - Giving bribes

(1) Whoever offers, gives or promises a bribe intended to that or another person to an official or responsible person to perform within or outside the limits of his authority an official or other action which he should not perform or not to perform an official or other action which he should perform, or whoever mediates in such bribery of an official or responsible person shall be punished by imprisonment for a term between one and eight years.

(2) Whoever offers, gives or promises a bribe intended to that or another person to an official or responsible person to perform an official or other action that he should perform, or not to perform an official or other action that he should not perform, within or outside the limits of his authority, or whoever mediates in such bribery of an official or responsible person shall be punished by imprisonment for a term between six months and five years.

(3) The perpetrator of the criminal offence referred to in paragraphs 1 and 2 of this Article who gave a bribe at the request of an official or responsible person and reported the offence before its discovery or before learning that the offence was discovered, may be released from punishment.

Article 296 - Giving bribes for trading in influence

(1) Whoever offers, promises or gives to another a bribe, intended for that or another person, to use his official or social position or influence to mediate the performance of an official or other action that should not be performed or not to perform an official or other action which should be performed shall be punished by imprisonment from one to eight years.

(2) Whoever offers, promises or gives to another a bribe, intended for that or another person, to use his official or social position or influence to mediate the performance of an official or other action that should be performed, or not to perform an official or other action which should not be performed shall be punished by imprisonment for a term between six months and five years.

(3) The perpetrator of the criminal offence referred to in paragraphs 1 and 2 of this Article who gave a bribe at the request of the person referred to in Article 295 of this Act and reported the offence before its discovery or before learning that the offence was discovered, may be released from punishment.

Provisions on sanctions and confiscation in the Criminal Act

Article 5

No one may retain the proceeds of an illegal act.

Article 40 - Types of penalties

1. Penalties are a fine, imprisonment and long-term imprisonment.
2. A fine may be imposed as a principal and as an ancillary penalty.
3. Imprisonment and long-term imprisonment may be imposed only as principal punishments.
4. When the law prescribes a prison sentence of up to three years for a certain criminal offence, the court may impose a fine as the main punishment.
5. For criminal offences committed out of greed, a fine may be imposed as an ancillary punishment even when it is not prescribed by law or when the law prescribes that the perpetrator shall be punished by imprisonment or a fine, and the court shall impose imprisonment as the main punishment.
6. Work for the common good shall be pronounced as a substitute for imprisonment or a fine.

Article 42 - Monetary fine

1. A fine shall be imposed in daily units. It may not be less than thirty or more than three hundred and sixty daily units, except for criminal offences committed out of greed, when up to five hundred daily units may be imposed or when a fine of five hundred daily units is expressly prescribed by this Act.
2. The judgment shall indicate the number of daily units and the amount of the daily amount and their product.
3. The number of daily units shall be determined on the basis of the circumstances specified in Article 47 of this Act, except for those relating to the property circumstances of the perpetrator.
4. The amount of the daily unit shall be determined taking into account the perpetrator's income and property and the average expenses necessary for the maintenance of the perpetrator and his family. The daily amount cannot be less than twenty kunas or more than ten thousand kunas.

[…]

Article 47 - Sentencing

1. When choosing the type and measure of punishment, the court shall, starting from the degree of guilt and the purpose of punishment, assess all circumstances that affect the punishment by type and measure to be lighter or heavier (mitigating and aggravating circumstances), and especially the severity of endangerment or violation of a legally protected good, the motives for the crime, the degree of violation of the perpetrator's duties, the manner of commission and the consequences of the crime, the perpetrator's previous life, his personal and financial circumstances and his behaviour after the crime, the relationship with the victim and the efforts to compensate.

2. The amount of the penalty may not exceed the degree of guilt.

Article 48 - Mitigation of punishment

1. The court may impose a sentence less severe than that prescribed for a certain criminal offence when the law explicitly prescribes it.

2. The court may also impose a milder punishment than prescribed for a certain criminal offence when there are special mitigating circumstances, especially if the perpetrator reconciled with the victim, if he fully or largely compensated the damage caused by the criminal offence or seriously tried to compensate that damage, and the purpose of punishment can be achieved by such a milder punishment.

3. The court may also impose a milder sentence than prescribed for a certain criminal offence when the state attorney and the defendant have agreed on it.

Article 50 - Exemption from punishment

1. The court may release the perpetrator from punishment:
   a. where such authority is based on an express statutory provision,
   b. when the consequences of a criminal offence committed through negligence affect him so severely that his punishment is unnecessary in order to achieve the purpose of punishment,
   c. when the perpetrator sought to eliminate or reduce the consequences of the criminal offence committed through negligence and compensated for the damage caused by it,
   d. when the perpetrator of the criminal offence for which only a fine or imprisonment of up to one year is prescribed has reconciled with the victim and compensated the damage.

2. When the court is authorized to release the perpetrator from punishment, it may also punish him more leniently, whereby it is not obliged to adhere to the limits prescribed in Article 49, paragraph 1 of this Act.

[…]

Article 77 – Conditions and manners of confiscation of the property gain

1. The property gain shall be confiscated by a court decision which has determined that an illegal action has been committed. Property gain will also be forfeited from the person to whom it is transferred if it is not acquired in good faith.

2. If the injured party has been awarded a property claim which, by its nature and content, corresponds to the obtained property gain, the part of the property gain that exceeds the awarded property claim shall be confiscated.

3. The court shall also confiscate the pecuniary benefit if it instructs the injured party that he may realize the property claim in litigation.

4. When it is determined that it is impossible to confiscate things or rights realized as property gain in whole or in part, the court shall order the perpetrator to pay the appropriate equivalent in the amount of money. Payment can be determined in instalments.

5. Confiscated property gain shall not be reduced by the amount of funds invested in criminal activity.

6. The court may decide that the property gain shall not be confiscated if it is insignificant.

[…]

Article 79 – Confiscation of items

1. Objects and assets created by the commission of a criminal offence shall be confiscated.

2. Objects and means that were intended or used for the commission of a criminal offence may be confiscated by the court.

3. The objects and means referred to in paragraphs 1 and 2 of this Article may also be confiscated by the court when the perpetrator of the unlawful act is not guilty.

4. Confiscated items and assets shall become the property of the Republic of Croatia. This does not affect the right of third parties to compensation from the perpetrator for the seized object or asset. The owner of a seized object or asset who is not the perpetrator has the right to return the object and asset or compensation of their market value from the state budget, unless he has at least through negligence contributed to the object or asset intended or used to commit a criminal offence, or if he has acquired the object or means knowing of the circumstances which enable its confiscation.

5. When the confiscation of an object or means is prescribed by law for a certain criminal offence, the owner shall not be entitled to compensation from the state budget, unless otherwise determined by a special law.

6. The court may order the destruction of the seized object or means.

Act on the Responsibility of Legal Persons for Criminal Offences

I. Basic provisions

Article 1

1. This Act determines the preconditions of liability, penalties, security measures, confiscation of property gain, confiscation of objects, public announcement of a judgment, statute of limitations and criminal proceedings for criminal offences of legal persons.

2. Legal persons within the meaning of this Act are also foreign persons who are considered legal persons under Croatian law.

Article 1a

This Act contains provisions that are in line with the following acts of the European Union:

- Council Framework Decision 2005/667 JHA, of 12 June 2005 to strengthen the criminal-law framework for the enforcement of the law against ship-source pollution (OJ L 255, 30. 9. 2005)
- Second Protocol of 19 June 1997, which was adopted on the basis of Article K.3 of the Treaty on European Union, to the Convention on the protection of the European Communities' financial interests (OJ C 221, 19. 7. 1997, p. 12).

Article 2 - Application of criminal law

Unless otherwise prescribed by this Act, the provisions of the Criminal Act, the Criminal Procedure Act and the Act on the Office for the Suppression of Corruption and Organized Crime shall apply to legal persons.

II. Conditions of liability

Article 3 - The basis of liability of legal persons

1. A legal person shall be punished for the criminal offence of a responsible person if it violates a duty of a legal person or with which the legal person has achieved or should have achieved an illegal property gain for itself or another.

2. Under the conditions referred to in paragraph 1 of this Article, a legal person shall be punished for criminal offences prescribed by the Criminal Act and other laws in which criminal offences are prescribed.

Article 4 - Responsible person

The responsible person in the sense of this Act is a natural person who manages the affairs of a legal person or is entrusted with the performance of activities in the field of activity of a legal person.

Article 5 – Attributing the fault of the responsible person to the legal person

1. The liability of a legal person shall be based on the fault of the responsible person.

2. A legal person shall also be punished for the criminal offence of a responsible person even in the case when the existence of legal or actual obstacles to determining the responsibility of the responsible person is established.

Article 6 - Exclusion and limitation of liability of legal persons

1. The Republic of Croatia, as a legal person, may not be punished for a criminal offence.

2. Units of local and regional self-government can be punished only for crimes that were not committed in the exercise of public authority.

Article 7 - Liability in case of change of legal person status

1. If a legal person ceases to exist before the criminal proceedings have ended, fines, security measures, public announcement of the judgment, confiscation of property gain and confiscation of items may be imposed on the legal person that is its general legal successor.

2. if a legal person ceases to exist after the final completion of the criminal proceedings, fines, security measures, public announcement of the judgment, confiscation of property gain and confiscation of items shall be executed in accordance with paragraph 1 of this Article.

3. A legal person in bankruptcy shall be punished for criminal offences committed before initiation or during the bankruptcy proceedings.

III. Penalties

Article 8 - Types of penalties

Penalties are a fine and termination of the legal person.

Article 9

Deleted.

Article 10 - Amount of the fine

1. If a fine or imprisonment with a special maximum term of one year is prescribed for a criminal offence, a legal person may be fined from HRK 5 000.00 to 8 000 000.00.

2. If the criminal offence is punishable by imprisonment with a special maximum term of five years, a legal person may be fined from HRK 15 000.00 to 10 000 000.00.

3. If the criminal offence is punishable by imprisonment with a special maximum termof ten years, the legal person may be fined from HRK 30 000.00 to HRK 12 000 000.00.

4. If the criminal offence is punishable by imprisonment with a special maximum term of fifteen years or a heavier sentence, the legal person may be fined from HRK 50 000.00 to HRK 15 000 000.00.

Article 10a - Execution of fines

If the legal person does not pay the fine within the specified period, the fine will be enforced.

Article 11 - Imposition of a fine for concurring criminal offences

If the court has imposed fines on a legal person for two or more concurring criminal offences, the single fine may not exceed the sum of the individual fines or the maximum legal measure of the fine.

Article 12 – Termination of a legal person

1. The penalty of termination of a legal person may be imposed if the legal person was established for the purpose of committing criminal offences or has used its activity predominantly to commit criminal offences.

2. The penalty of termination of a legal person may not be imposed on local and regional self-government units and political parties.

3. In addition to the penalty of termination of a legal person, the court may also impose a fine.

4. After the judgment on the termination of a legal person becomes final, the liquidation of the legal person shall be carried out.

Article 12a - Exemption from punishment

A legal person who reported the criminal offence of a responsible person before its discovery or before learning that the offence has been discovered, may be released from punishment.

Article 13 - Probation

1. The court may pronounce a suspended sentence on the legal person instead of a fine and simultaneously determine that the fine shall not be collected if the legal person does not commit another criminal offence within the time specified by the court, which may not be shorter than one or longer than three years.

2. A suspended sentence may be imposed for criminal offences for which the court has sentenced a legal person to a fine of less than HRK 50,000.00.

3. A partial suspended sentence may not be applied to a legal person.

Article 14

Deleted.

III.a Security measures

Article 15 - Types of security measures

Apart from other penalties the court may impose one or more of the following security measures on the legal person: ban on performing certain activities or jobs, ban on obtaining licenses, authorizations, concessions or subsidies, ban on business with state and local budgets, and forfeiture.

Article 16 - Prohibition to perform certain activities or jobs

1. The prohibition of performing certain activities or jobs may be imposed in respect of one or more activities or jobs in the performance of which the offence was committed.

2. The court may impose a ban on performing certain activities or jobs on a legal person for a period of one to three years, counting from the finality of the judgment if further performance of certain activities or jobs would be dangerous to life, health or safety of people or property, or the economy, or if the legal person has already been convicted of the same or a similar criminal offence.

3. A ban on performing certain activities or jobs may not be imposed on local and regional self-government units and political parties.

Article 17 - Prohibition to obtain permits, authorizations, concessions or subsidies

1. The court may impose a ban on the acquisition of permits, authorizations, concessions or subsidies issued by state bodies or units of local and regional self-government to a legal person if there is a danger that such acquisition of permits, authorizations, concessions or subsidies could have an incentive effect on the commission of a new criminal offence.

2. The security measure referred to in paragraph 1 of this Article shall be pronounced for a period of one to three years, counting from the finality of the court judgment.

Article 18 – Prohibition from doing business with users of state and local budgets

1. A ban on doing business with users of the state and local budgets may be imposed on a legal person if there is a danger that such business could have an incentive effect on the commission of a new criminal offence.

2. The security measure referred to in paragraph 1 of this Article shall be pronounced for a period of one to three years, counting from the finality of the court judgment.

III.b Seizure of property, seizure of items and public announcement of judgment

Article 19 - Confiscation of property gains and confiscation of items

The provisions of the Criminal Act and special laws shall apply to confiscation of property gain and confiscation of objects.

Article 20

Deleted.

Article 21 - Public announcement of the judgment

1. The court may order the public announcement of a judgment when, given the significance of the criminal offence, it determines that there are justified reasons to inform the public about the final judgment.

2. The court shall order that the judgment be published in whole or in part, and the time limit within which it must be published. A publicly announced judgment may contain the name of the injured party but only with his/her consent.

3. The court shall determine in which media the judgment referred to in paragraph 1 of this Article shall be published. The media will publish the said judgment at the expense of the convicted legal persons.

www.ingramcontent.com/pod-product-compliance
Lightning Source LLC
Chambersburg PA
CBHW080620270326
41928CB00016B/3142